THE UNITED NATIONS

Also by Sydney D. Bailey

WAR AND CONSCIENCE IN THE NUCLEAR AGE
CHRISTIAN PERSPECTIVES ON NUCLEAR WEAPONS
HOW WARS END (2 vols)
THE MAKING OF RESOLUTION 242
THE PROCEDURE OF THE UN SECURITY COUNCIL
VOTING IN THE UN SECURITY COUNCIL
THE GENERAL ASSEMBLY OF THE UNITED NATIONS
THE SECRETARIAT OF THE UNITED NATIONS
BRITISH PARLIAMENTARY DEMOCRACY
CEYLON
FOUR ARAB–ISRAELI WARS AND THE PEACE PROCESS
PARLIAMENTARY GOVERNMENT IN SOUTHERN ASIA
NAISSANCE DE NOUVELLES DEMOCRATIES
PEACEFUL SETTLEMENTS OF INTERNATIONAL DISPUTES
THE KOREAN ARMISTICE
PEACE IS A PROCESS
THE UN SECURITY COUNCIL AND HUMAN RIGHTS

Edited by Sydney D. Bailey

HUMAN RIGHTS AND RESPONSIBILITIES IN BRITAIN
    AND IRELAND
ASPECTS OF AMERICAN GOVERNMENT
THE BRITISH PARTY SYSTEM
PROBLEMS OF PARLIAMENTARY GOVERNMENT IN
    COLONIES
PARLIAMENTARY GOVERNMENT IN THE
    COMMONWEALTH
THE FUTURE OF THE HOUSE OF LORDS

Also by Sam Daws

PREVENTIVE DIPLOMACY
MEMORANDUM ON AN AGENDA FOR PEACE

The United Nations

A Concise Political Guide

Sydney D. Bailey

and

Sam Daws

Third Edition

Barnes & Noble Books

First published 1963 (by Pall Mall (London) and Frederick A. Praeger
(New York) as *A Short Political Guide to the United Nations*)
Second edition (*The United Nations: A Short Political Guide*) 1989
Third edition (*The United Nations: A Concise Political Guide*) 1995

Published in Great Britain by
MACMILLAN PRESS LTD
Houndmills, Basingstoke, Hampshire RG21 2XS
and London
Companies and representatives
throughout the world

A catalogue record for this book is available
from the British Library.

ISBN 0–333–62916–7 hardcover
ISBN 0–333–62917–5 paperback

10   9   8   7   6   5   4   3   2   1
04   03   02   01   00   99   98   97   96   95

Printed in Great Britain by
Ipswich Book Co Ltd
Ipswich, Suffolk

First published in the United States of America 1995 by
BARNES & NOBLE BOOKS
4720 Boston Way
Lanham, MD 20706

Library of Congress Cataloging-in-Publication Data
Bailey, Sydney Dawson.
The United Nations : a concise political guide / Sydney D. Bailey
and Sam Daws. — 3rd ed.
p.   cm.
Includes bibliographical references and index.
ISBN 0–389–21012–9
1. United Nations.   I. Daws, Sam.
JX1977.8225   1995
341.23—dc20   94–35666
                                                    CIP

Contents

List of Tables

Acknowledgements

We are indebted to the libraries at the Royal Institute of International Affairs and the UN Information Centre in London, whose staffs have been unfailingly helpful. We are also grateful for the assistance of Comfort Ero and to Diane Jumet and to Solange Habib, who responded cheerfully and promptly to our many requests.

Sydney D. Bailey and Sam Daws
June 1994

1 Purposes

Human beings think of anarchy and despotism as opposites, and fear them both equally. A system of law and justice is a bulwark against the two extremes, and the inadequacy of this system governing the relations among nations is one reason why human life is precarious. The one unilateral policy that we expect from our government is to pursue the national interest; but to do this without taking account of the legitimate interests of others will soon lead to conflict, perhaps even armed conflict.

It is no longer fashionable in the West to glorify war – but to say with General Sherman that war is hell is merely to strike an attitude. War as an instrument of national policy will disappear when nations no longer quarrel, or when there are effective and trusted non-violent means of resolving differences. Some of these means of settling disputes peacefully are listed in the UN Charter (Art. 33): negotiation, mediation, arbitration, judicial settlement, and the like.

Because human beings are potentially both selfish and altruistic, government is a mixture of consent and coercion. Law-breaking in national society is restrained by three kinds of force: the force of the police, the force of public opinion, and the force of personal conscience. Breaches of the law are supposedly deterred or punished through an impartial system of justice. Provocation, however intense, does not authorize citizens to take the law into their own hands. It is no defence to a charge of murder to say that the victim was odious.

International coercion in support of law is both more difficult and more dangerous than coercion in support of national law. It is more difficult because international law is still relatively rudimentary, and nations do not yet feel the same obligation to respect what international law there is, as most citizens in democracies feel to observe

1

national law. It is more dangerous because any use of coercive armed force may escalate. All-out war with the most modern weapons would be too destructive and too indiscriminate to serve as an instrument of justice.

There have, broadly speaking, been two approaches in the attempt to limit or abolish resort to armed force in settling international disputes. Some have considered war to be an outward manifestation of inward human wickedness which will be abolished if people become more moral or more enlightened. They have stressed personal conduct and the power of example. A few have adopted a wholly pacifist position and have refused all personal participation in war or its preparation.

Others have regarded war as a social institution which can be eliminated in the present state of human imperfection by improving the methods and institutions for preventing or resolving international disputes. Civilized people no longer practise cannibalism or slavery, though the heart of man is no less deceitful and desperately wicked than it was in the time of Jeremiah. Unless human beings abolish war, it is said, war will abolish human beings.

We do not know for certain whether war can be abolished; and if it can, whether it will be because human beings have become more moral and enlightened, or because they have invented better techniques for its avoidance. William Penn, the Anglo-American Quaker who pioneered the idea of an international organization for making and keeping peace, maintained that 'though good laws do well, good men do better'.

The main purpose of the United Nations, as it was of the League of Nations, is to ensure that armed force is not used, save in the common interest. UN Members are supposed to settle international disputes peacefully (a positive obligation) and not to threaten the territorial integrity or political independence of other states (a negative obligation). These are far-reaching commitments, for they may mean that the only unilateral use of armed force that is permissible to UN members is in self-defence in response to an armed attack. When the Nazi leaders were charged at Nürnberg with having waged aggressive war, it was no defence to say that Germany had grievances. The founders of the United Nations established a two-fold system for peace. On the one hand, nations wishing to join the Organization had to accept the high standards of international conduct contained in the UN Charter, including

- agreement that UN obligations take precedence over all other international obligations (Art. 103);
- renunciation of the use of force, except in self-defence after an armed attack (a unilateral use of armed force) or in UN action to maintain or restore peace and security (a multilateral use of armed force) (Arts. 2(4), 42, and 51);
- settlement of international disputes by peaceful means only (Arts. 2(3) and 33);
- international cooperation to ensure respect for human rights and fundamental freedoms, including the principle of equal rights and self-determination of peoples (Arts. 1(2) and (3), and 55);
- recognition of the sovereign equality of states (Art. 2(1));
- the UN not to intervene in the domestic matters of states, except when it is applying enforcement measures under Chapter VII (Art. 2(7));
- agreement to cooperate with other states in accordance with the UN Charter (Art. 1(3));
- fulfilment of the other obligations of the UN Charter, including the obligation to accept and carry out the decisions of the Security Council, which acts on behalf of all UN Members (Arts. 2, 24(1), 25, and 49).

This is bland diplomatic jargon, to be sure, and the challenge in the closing years of the twentieth century is to convert the universally agreed principles into acceptable policies.

The second aspect of maintaining peace envisaged by the founders was the creation of machinery to deal with the situation which would arise if nations failed to honour their obligations not to threaten or use force. It was intended at the founding conference in San Francisco that the collective strength of all should be used to deter or punish aggression. National armed forces were to be reduced, and the Security Council was to dispose of military units for joint action, subject only to the veto of the five permanent members of the Security Council. These aims were never realized, ostensibly because of the failure of the five permanent members of the Security Council to agree on the types, scale and control of forces and facilities to be placed at the disposal of the Council. Instead of the fully-fledged system of collective security outlined in the Charter, the United Nations has operated pragmatically with procedures designed to respond to each situation on an *ad hoc* basis through peace-keeping and similar operations.

In order to achieve the purposes of the UN, six 'principal organs' were created, as follows (Art. 7(1)):

- a General Assembly consisting of all UN Members, with almost unlimited deliberative powers, and limited powers to recommend action or take binding decisions (Arts. 9–22);
- three Councils of limited membership to deal with peace and security (Arts. 23–54), economic and social questions (Arts. 55–72), and the international trusteeship system (Arts. 75–91);
- an international Secretariat headed by a Secretary-General, recruited on as wide a geographical basis as possible (Arts. 97 and 101);
- an International Court of Justice composed of 15 independent judges (Arts. 92–6 of the Charter and Articles 2–3 of the Statute of the Court).

Under the four policymaking organs are a great many subsidiary bodies reporting to the parent Council or the General Assembly, annually or as necessary (Arts. 7(2), 22, 29, 68).

Related to the United Nations are a number of autonomous inter-governmental agencies. Some deal with technical co-operation, such as the International Atomic Energy Agency (headquarters in Vienna) and the International Civil Aviation Organization (Montreal), while others are concerned with welfare and standard-setting, such as the World Health Organization (Geneva) and the International Labour Organization (Geneva). The International Bank for Reconstruction and Development (World Bank) and the International Monetary Fund (IMF), and their affiliated organizations, are also specialized agencies of the UN. GATT (the General Agreement on Tariffs and Trade), is not a UN-related agency but could become one if an appropriate organization were created to administer the Agreement.

The smallest (and oldest) of these agencies is the Universal Postal Union (UPU), with a staff of 171 in 1993 and an annual budget of £13 million. The states and territories which belong to the UPU are regarded as forming a single postal region in which mail is handled on a reciprocal basis. The members accept standard regulations for postal charges, weights and sizes, and there are other agreements for more complicated services, such as cash-on-delivery parcels. The largest agency is the Food and Agriculture Organization (FAO) which employs 6100 persons (including field staff) and had a budget of over £400 million for the biennium 1993–4. The FAO's function is to improve production and distribution of agricultural products worldwide and to better the living conditions of rural people.

The United Nations is supposed to coordinate the policies and activities of the agencies, but there is in practice very little coordination, as the agencies have their own governing bodies and budgets. The United Nations' regular budget totalled $1.1 billion for 1994 and the agencies almost double this figure. The British share of these budgets varies. The UK contributes 2.5 per cent of the International Maritime Organization budget but 5 per cent of the budget of the International Telecommunications Union.

There are also five regional economic commissions (in

two cases dealing also with social affairs) and two long-term peace observation missions (in the Middle East and Kashmir), financed from the regular UN budget. There are peace-keeping and observer missions in various areas of tension, financed by ordinary budgetary assessments or special arrangements. A UN peace-keeping force in Sinai (UNEF II) was withdrawn in 1982 and replaced by a non-UN operation, after threat of a Soviet veto because of opposition to the Camp David accords. Finally, there are ten agencies established by the General Assembly but financed mainly by voluntary governmental contributions rather than from assessed contributions to the regular UN budget, dealing with such matters as economic development, the care of refugees, the protection of the environment, and population issues.

Some of the extra-budgetary activities have continued almost as long as the United Nations itself. The agency for Palestine refugees, for example, was established after the 1948 war in the Middle East and now cares for more than two-and-a-half million Palestinian refugees in Lebanon, Syria, Jordan, the West Bank and the Gaza Strip, at an annual cost of more than $250 million. The truce supervision mission in the Middle East was established by the UN mediator in 1948.

The cost of these activities to the ordinary citizen can be expressed in various ways. The Universal Postal Union costs the United Kingdom citizen just over one penny a year. Britain's share of the regular annual budget of the United Nations is less than one-five-hundredth of its annual expenditure on military defence.

The pace of history is fast, and is accelerating. The world of the 1990s is very different from that envisaged by the founders of the UN. The development of weapons of massive and indiscriminate destruction has shaken Clausewitz's pre-nuclear axiom that war is simply a continuation of diplomacy by other means. National defence forces may not always deter, for governments do not always act wisely or respond rationally, and not all wars follow from calculated decisions. There is no easy escape from the risk of war by misunderstanding or miscalculation. Some powers have in their armouries too many weapons that are more effective if used first than second. Stability may be upset by political re-alignment or technological breakthrough. The rapid obsolescence of weapons induces a frantic search for new weapons systems, so that to win the arms race becomes an end in itself.

Those who created the United Nations could not foresee the age of long-range missiles which can destroy the enemy's homeland without first defeating the intervening army: but war with the weapons we now call conventional was already barbaric in 1945. The aim now is not to make war more civilized but to render it redundant.

The San Francisco Charter always had flaws. Moreover, issues have arisen which the founders could not have foreseen. The Charter refers cautiously to the regulation of armaments, 'and possible disarmament' (Art. 47), but few states have undertaken substantial disarmament, whether unilaterally or by international agreement.

A UN Register of Conventional Arms came into effect in January 1992, but states have not yet agreed to reduce their stocks of conventional weapons. This is in spite of the fact that these are the weapons that have predominantly been used in some 200 'small' wars since 1945.

The process of decolonization has had an important effect on the working of the United Nations. The need for this was foreseen in 1945, but not the speed. Its most spectacular manifestation for the United Nations has been in the changed composition of the General Assembly. In 1945 the Members from Africa numbered four: today there are 52. Asia has increased from eight to 46, and 13 former colonies in the Caribbean area have achieved independence and UN Membership since 1945. Almost 100 territories have been decolonized since the foundation of the United Nations.

This increase in Membership has meant a radical shift in the balance of votes in UN organs. Former colonies now command a majority of votes in the main UN organs – though decisions of the General Assembly on important

TABLE 1.1   UN Membership, 1945–1 January 1994

Year	Western Europe	Eastern Europe	Africa	Asia and the Pacific	Latin America and the Caribbean	United States, Older Commonwealth	TOTAL
Founder Members	9	6	4	8	20	4	51
Admitted during							
1946	2	–	–	2	–	–	55
1947	–	–	–	2	–	–	57
1948	–	–	–	1	–	–	58
1949	–	–	–	1	–	–	59
1950	–	–	–	1	–	–	60
1951	–	–	–	–	–	–	60
1952	–	–	–	–	–	–	60
1953	–	–	–	–	–	–	60
1954	–	–	–	–	–	–	60
1955	6	4	1	5	–	–	76
1956	–	–	3	1	–	–	80
1957	–	–	1	1	–	–	82
1958	–	–	1	–	–	–	83
1959	–	–	–	–	–	–	83
1960	–	–	16	1	–	–	100
1961	–	–	3	1	–	–	104
1962	–	–	4	–	2	–	110
1963	–	–	2	1	–	–	113
1964	1	–	1	–	–	–	115
1965	–	–	1	2	–	–	118
1966	–	–	2	1	2	–	123
1967	–	–	–	–	–	–	123
1968	–	–	3	–	–	–	126
1969	–	–	–	–	–	–	126
1970	–	–	–	1	–	–	127
1971	–	–	–	5	–	–	132
1972	–	–	–	–	–	–	132
1973	1	1	–	–	1	–	135
1974	–	–	1	1	1	–	138
1975	–	–	4	1	1	–	144
1976	–	–	2	1	–	–	147
1977	–	–	1	1	–	–	149
1978	–	–	–	1	1	–	151
1979	–	–	–	–	1	–	152
1980	–	–	1	–	1	–	154
1981	–	–	–	1	2	–	157
1982	–	–	–	–	–	–	157
1983	–	–	–	–	1	–	158
1984	–	–	–	1	–	–	159

Year	Western Europe	Eastern Europe	Africa	Asia and the Pacific	Latin America and the Caribbean	United States, Older Commonwealth	TOTAL
1985	–	–	–	–	–	–	159
1986	–	–	–	–	–	–	159
1987	–	–	–	–	–	–	159
1988	–	–	–	–	–	–	159
1989	–	–	–	–	–	–	159
1990	1	–1	1	–1	–	–	159
1991	–	3	–	4	–	–	166
1992	1	12	–	–	–	–	179
1993	2	2	1	–	–	–	184
TOTAL	23	27	53	44	33	4	184

Serbia and Montenegro (formerly Yugoslavia) is included in this table, although its participation in certain UN activities was suspended when we went to press.

questions require a two-thirds vote, and it is not possible to make substantive decisions in the Security Council if there is a negative vote by one or more of the five permanent members.

The increase in the Organization's Membership has meant that business takes longer: annual sessions of the General Assembly now last months rather than weeks. It is not that representatives of the new nations are exceptionally long-winded, but simply that there are nearly four times as many Members as there were in 1945.

But the most far-reaching consequence of the changed composition of the United Nations does not lie in the fact of numbers but in the character and interests of the nations admitted since 1946. Many are former dependencies of Western powers, sensitive about manifestations of racial prejudice or discrimination, proud of their newly-won nationhood. Most of them are relatively poor and underdeveloped but aim to achieve in decades the economic and social advances which elsewhere took centuries. They reject the bland assumption that the world should be run in accordance with the principles of the industrialized North.

They are not powerful in the conventional sense, but

some of them aspire to major-power status in the future. Until recently they placed great faith in the United Nations precisely because it seeks to minimize the role of national power, but they are fearful that a more active UN may in the future be dominated by a few powerful states.

The concentration of voting power in the hands of relatively weak nations distorts the realities of the international situation. More than half of UN Members contribute 0.01 per cent each to the UN regular budget (see Appendix 2). A two-thirds majority vote in the General Assembly can in theory be secured by states which together contribute less than 3 per cent of the UN budget.

Apart from the Security Council, there can be no guarantee that UN organs will not take decisions by a coalition of the weak and the irresponsible. That is a risk inherent in any political system in which differences are resolved by voting. Lord Salisbury once described democracy as 'a system by which the rich pay all the taxes and the poor make all the laws'.

The use of voting to settle international questions is one manifestation of conference diplomacy, or parliamentary diplomacy, as it was labelled by Dean Rusk. This new form of diplomacy has four main features; first, public debate of issues not only by the parties or other interested nations, but by all Members who happen to belong to the organ in question at any particular time; second, termination of debate by a formal conclusion usually reached by voting; third, agreed rules and practices which are subject to tactical manipulation to advance or oppose a point of view; and fourth, an ongoing organization with interests and responsibilities more extensive than the specific items which happen to be on the agenda of an organ at any particular time.

This parliamentary diplomacy differs greatly from traditional diplomacy. The essence of old-style diplomacy was that it was invariably conducted in private. When the rules of procedure of the Security Council were being drafted in 1945, several delegates objected to the proposal that the Council should occasionally meet in private. It was said that one of the main purposes of the United Nations was to minimize secret diplomacy: for the Security Council to meet in private, suggested Syria, would be unconstitutional and contrary to the Charter. Norway pointed out, on the other hand, that if closed meetings were not allowed, delicate issues would be discussed in informal meetings, and this would tend to even greater secrecy. It took three meetings before a rule of procedure could be agreed, and this provided that the Security Council should be allowed to meet in private if it so wished.

Increasingly in recent years, formal open meetings of the Council have been preceded by informal consultations or closed meetings, sometimes of the United States and the Russian Federation, sometimes of the three Western permanent members, sometimes of all five permanent members, occasionally of all 15 members of the Council. When this happens, the formal open meeting simply endorses what has been agreed in private. The advantage of this is that it avoids the participation of non-members and polemical speechmaking which is so often a necessary part of public debate. On the other hand, many non-Council UN Members are uneasy that private decision-making conceals improper pressures and bargains, so that issues are not decided on merit but on the whim of one or two Members.

Perhaps the first person to breach the tradition that diplomacy should always be secret was Leon Trotsky, at the Brest-Litovsk peace conference in 1918, when he directed his words, not to the diplomats across the table, but to 'the war-weary workers of all countries'. Many speeches at the United Nations are to satisfy public opinion at home or to court uncommitted opinion abroad, not to influence the other diplomats in the room who are listening (or pretending to listen).

Public opinion is nowadays concerned with international affairs to an extent that would have astonished the practitioners of traditional diplomacy. Open covenants of peace are desirable and they are often openly arrived at. In his history of the war between Athens and Sparta, Thucydides gives several examples of a diplomatic envoy stating his case directly to the people of another state. That is now a commonplace of parliamentary diplomacy.

Decisions in traditional diplomacy were unanimous, which meant that a dissatisfied party had the power of veto. At the San Francisco conference in 1945, the great powers justified the veto in the Security Council by pointing out that the right they were claiming was not new. This was to miss the point, however, because the medium and smaller powers were not complaining that the veto was an innovation: they wanted to know why, if the veto was such a good thing, the right was being granted only to five powers.

A UN vote is useful if it registers agreement already reached or induces a situation in which agreement is more likely in the future. A vote which merely registers disagreement serves little useful purpose – except, perhaps, to satisfy the sponsors and enable the body concerned to pass to the next item of business. Many contentious proposals are pressed to a vote in UN organs, and this tends to perpetuate disagreement rather than persuade the minority to change their opinions or actions. A two-thirds vote in the General Assembly to recommend sanctions against a state which violates human rights, but which does not include the votes of the countries with the economic power to make sanctions effective, may lull uneasy consciences; it may assert important principles; it may establish crucial precedents; it may even create an impression that progress has been made; but it has failed in an essential purpose if it has not helped to modify the views, or at least the actions, of those in a position to change the situation that has aroused concern.

Debate is often more influential than the vote with which it normally terminates. Charges can be denied, grievances articulated, claims asserted, accusations rebutted, initiatives launched. The difficulty is that speeches are directed to several different audiences at the same time. A speech made to intimidate a foreign adversary may have the effect of agitating public opinion at home. The perfect speech would demonstrate to the home audience that the government is vigorously pursuing the national interest in face of foreign provocation, but at the same time would have two other effects: to persuade the self-same foreigners that the government is firm in its resolve but eager to reach an honourable settlement, and convince uncommitted opinion that the government's goal is reasonable and its methods conciliatory.

Decisions of UN organs come in course of time to represent new international norms. All nations pay some heed to UN resolutions – some more than others. The UN machinery of investigation, peacemaking, or coercion is there in the background, to be used or not as the Members decide. Leaders who have embarked on risky courses of action and want a plausible reason for pulling back can say that they are doing so out of respect for international opinion, as evidenced in the deliberations and decisions of UN organs.

Some international crises get out of hand because events move too fast and there is insufficient time to take stock. UN diplomacy can appear cumbersome, but this is not always a disadvantage. The Western airlift to Berlin in 1948 was at first intended as a stopgap measure to buy time for diplomatic discussions, and this was buttressed by a month's formal debate and informal discussions at the United Nations. Indeed, the issue was eventually sorted out following a seemingly casual conversation between US and Soviet diplomats in the delegates' lounge at UN Headquarters in New York.

The development of the Cuban missile crisis in 1962 was slowed down by an intensive exchange of diplomatic messages between US and Soviet heads of government and by the activities of the UN Security Council. Tedious and barely relevant speeches at the United Nations provide convenient opportunities for diplomatic negotiations: one Saudi Arabian diplomat, the late Jamil Baroody, could always be depended on to speak, whatever the subject, if time were needed for private conversations or there were good reasons for delaying a decision.

On the other hand, time is of service only if it is put to good use. The Middle East slid into war in 1967 in spite of the fact that the Security Council had spent the previous fortnight actively considering the matters at issue, and no amount of diplomatic activity was able to prevent the Bangladesh war in 1971. Moreover, some crises erupt with little warning, as with the Argentine assault on the Falklands–Malvinas in 1982, or Iraq's invasion and attempted annexation of Kuwait in 1990.

So far, we have been looking at the United Nations through a wide-angle lens. In the next chapter we zoom in on the UN structure and look at the details in close-up.

2 Structure

The United Nations was set up as a successor to the League of Nations by the victors in the Second World War. Only those states which declared war on the Axis powers were regarded as peace-loving and so invited to the founding conference. The Soviet Government had earlier asked that the 16 republics then constituting the Soviet Union should have separate Membership in the United Nations. President Roosevelt countered by saying that he would ask for Membership for the 48 states then forming the United States. At the summit conference at Yalta, the Soviet Union agreed to modify its original demand and to accept three seats in the Organization, in exchange for American concessions regarding the veto in the Security Council. In addition to the Soviet Union, therefore, the Byelorussian and Ukrainian Soviet Socialist Republics became founding Members of the United Nations. Fifty delegations from 48 countries participated in the San Francisco conference, and Poland subsequently became a founder Member.

The San Francisco conference was formally sponsored by China, the Soviet Union, the United Kingdom, and the United States, and these four submitted a draft Charter which had been prepared at a preliminary conference at Dumbarton Oaks. France was invited to be a 'sponsoring power' at San Francisco but declined: General de Gaulle was piqued at not having been invited to the Yalta conference, and France had not shared in drafting the Dumbarton Oaks proposals.

The San Francisco conference opened on 25 April 1945, the day on which Western and Soviet troops met on the Elbe. Within ten days Nazi Germany had surrendered. Two months later the Charter was ready for signature.

The Charter provided that Membership in the United Nations would be open to all peace-loving states which accept the obligations of the Charter and, 'in the judgment of the Organization, are able and willing to carry out these obligations'. Admission, suspension and expulsion of Members would be by 'the General Assembly upon the recommendation of the Security Council' (Arts. 4 to 6 of the Charter): if the Security Council makes no recommendation, the General Assembly is powerless to act. Decisions on Membership now require the affirmative votes of the five permanent members and at least four other members of the Security Council, and a two-thirds majority in the General Assembly (Arts. 18(2) and 27(3)).

There were originally two concepts of UN Membership. It was argued, on the one hand, that because the United Nations is committed to certain high principles of international conduct, only those states clearly willing to accept and honour the obligations of the Charter qualify for Membership. The United Nations, according to this view, is a club. Nobody should be compelled to join: standards for admission should be high.

The other view was more pragmatic. If the United Nations is to be effective, it was argued, it needs the participation of all, or virtually all, of the sovereign nations. Few UN Members have consistently lived up to the high standards of the Charter. The only test of the suitability of an applicant, it was said, should be whether the entity is a state or not.

The second view increasingly came to prevail, especially after the package-deal of admissions in 1955. It is still a matter of form for a state applying for admission to declare that it accepts the obligations of the Charter, but there is little serious attempt to judge the ability or willingness of the applicant state to carry out these obligations. The Security Council, normally without much debate, adopts a resolution along the following lines.

The Security Council,
Having examined the application of . . . for admission to the United Nations,
Recommends to the General Assembly that . . . be admitted to membership in the United Nations.

The General Assembly, on a convenient occasion, receives the recommendation and, by acclamation, admits the applicant state to Membership.

Most sovereign states belong to the United Nations. Switzerland has not applied to join, believing that Membership involves an obligation to use collective force against aggression, which would be inconsistent with Swiss neutrality. Three very small states (Nauru, Tonga, and Tuvalu) are not Members but participate in some UN activities. Eighteen other dependent territories have not yet exercised self-determination (see Appendix 3).

The two views about Membership of the United Nations are well illustrated by the debates over the issue of Chinese representation. The Republic of China is a founder Member of the United Nations and is named in the Charter as a permanent member of the Security Council (Art. 23(1)). When Chiang Kai-shek was driven from the Chinese mainland and took refuge in Taiwan, the question was bound to arise whether China should in future be represented in United Nations organs by the new Communist government in China or the nationalist regime in Taiwan, since both claimed to be 'the Republic of China'. This question had both political and constitutional aspects: the political arguments went something like this.

The United States, supported by some of its friends and allies, maintained that the Chinese government in Peking (Beijing) did not represent the true will and aspirations of the Chinese people. It had shown brutality and lack of morality, both internally and internationally. It committed aggression in Korea, destroyed the autonomy of Tibet, invaded India, fostered subversion in South East Asia and elsewhere, and threatened to attack Taiwan. Communist China, according to this view, was not peace-loving. To admit its representatives to the United Nations would disrupt the Organization, reduce the prospects for successful action against aggression in the future, and be interpreted by free nations everywhere as an abandonment of their cause. Representatives of the nationalist regime in Taiwan had served the United Nations loyally and should not be expelled.

The Communist states, on the other hand, maintained that the United States had never reconciled itself to the victory of popular revolution in China, but had tried to thwart the will of the Chinese people by depriving China of its rightful place in the United Nations. The United States, it was said, had seized Taiwan and turned it into a base for aggression against the People's Republic of China. If US forces were removed from Taiwan, the Chiang Kai-shek regime would be swept aside. The Chinese seat at the United Nations had been occupied by those who represented nobody. The United Nations should have no concern with internal developments in China. All that mattered was that China was a peace-loving state, had always pursued a policy of peaceful co-existence, and had concluded treaties of friendship and non-aggression with other nations.

Several non-Communist governments, including the UK, India and the Scandinavian countries, took a pragmatic position. They held that the Chinese seat in UN organs should be occupied by representatives of the Chinese People's Republic because that government effectively controlled the national territory. They maintained that the character of the government had no bearing on the question of representation in United Nations organs: other governments had disregarded the obligations of the Charter, but this had not interfered with their Membership. If the People's Republic of China represented a threat to world peace, it was preferable for it to be present in the United Nations rather than excluded.

These political views influenced the way UN Members dealt with the constitutional issue. If the People's Republic of China had specifically applied for United Nations Membership, the question of admission would have been considered in the ordinary way by the Security Council and, in the event of a positive recommendation by the Council, by the General Assembly. Such a procedure might, of course, have run into a US veto in the Security Council. In the absence of an application for Membership, however, the issue was one of representation rather than Membership: which government, in other words, was entitled to issue credentials for 'the Republic of China'.

The United States exerted enormous diplomatic pressure, first to postpone the issue and then to ensure that, whenever the question came to a vote in the General Assembly, it would be regarded as 'important' and therefore require a two-thirds majority vote for a decision (Art. 18(2)). Finally, in 1971, the General Assembly decided 'to restore all its rights to the People's Republic of China . . . and to expel forthwith the representatives of Chiang Kai-shek . . .'.

The General Assembly is the one UN organ to which all UN Members belong (Art. 9). It convenes for its ordinary annual session in September; if, as is now often the case, business is not completed by about the third week in December, the session resumes the following year. The Assembly has also met 18 times in special session and nine times in emergency special session (Art. 20). The Assembly meets in plenary meeting to elect officers and for other procedural business, for a general debate lasting about a month, and for certain substantive items of special importance. A committee of the Assembly reviews all proposals to place items on the agenda, makes recommendations regarding the date for adjourning or closing the session, and is supposed to assist the President of the Assembly in the discharge of his responsibilities. Nowadays the Assembly has more than 170 items on its annual agenda, though some of these overlap.

Most substantive items requiring debate and decision are first considered in public in one or other of six main committees of the whole Membership. Procedure in these committees is less formal than in the plenary. Representatives speak seated at their desks rather than standing at a rostrum at the front, and voting is by simple majority. All recommendations approved in committee are later considered in the plenary, where a two-thirds vote is necessary for deciding important questions (Art. 18).

The General Assembly transacts three types of business:

(i) In a few matters, the Assembly has exclusive authority: the most important of these are control of the budget, apportionment of the expenses of the United Nations, and elections to the three Councils (Arts. 17, 19, 23(1), 61(1) and 86(1)).

(ii) In certain other matters, the Assembly can take a decision only if there is a recommendation from the Security Council. These matters include the appointment of the Secretary-General, United Nations Membership, and amendments to the Charter (Arts. 4(2), 5, 6, 97 and 108). In these matters the Assembly has in practice acted as a rubber-stamp. The Assembly and the Security Council are jointly responsible for electing the judges of the International Court of Justice (Art. 8 of the Statute of the Court).

(iii) In addition, the Assembly has wide powers of debate concerning matters within the scope of the Charter, and the right to initiate studies, make recommendations, or express opinions (Arts. 10 to 15 of the Charter).

Of the three UN Councils, the Security Council is the best-known. It consists of five permanent members (the Republic of China, France, the Russian Federation, the United Kingdom and the United States), each with the right of veto on most kinds of substantive decision, and ten other members (originally six) elected by the General Assembly (Art. 23), since 1965 in accordance with an agreed geographical formula. The Security Council is in theory very powerful. All Members of the UN have agreed that the Council has 'primary responsibility' for maintaining peace and 'acts on their behalf', and all have undertaken to accept and carry out its decisions (Arts. 24(1), 25, and 49).

The Council is able to meet at short notice; indeed, the Charter states that it shall be so organized as to be able to 'function continuously' (Art. 28(1)). It is laid down in the rules of procedure that the Council shall meet at least once every 14 days, but the members usually agree not to apply the rule. The Charter provides for occasional meetings at foreign minister or similar level (Art. 28(2)). Between the foundation of the United Nations and the end of 1993, the Council held 3325 meetings. The Security Council usually meets at United Nations Headquarters in New York, but it can meet elsewhere if it so decides (Art. 28(3)).

The Security Council now operates in six languages: Arabic, Chinese, English, French, Spanish and Russian. Simultaneous interpretation by headphones is provided by the Secretariat into these languages. One diplomat, Victor Andres Belaunde of Peru, used to choose a language to suit his mood: French when he wanted to be precise, English when he wanted to understate, Spanish when he wanted to exaggerate.

Non-members of the Council may ask to participate in the debates, but if they initiate proposals, these are put to a vote only if a Council member so requests, and non-members are not entitled to vote (Arts. 31–2). Non-members have taken advantage of this provision, especially over Southern Africa. In 1983 no fewer than 63 non-members took part in one debate. The Council has increasingly used informal methods of private consultation before a public meeting is convened, such consultations usually being initiated by the President for the month.

One of the most distinctive features of the Security Council, however, is that it is the only United Nations organ in which there is a formal rule of unanimity, or right of veto. The Charter declares that decisions of the Council shall be by the affirmative vote of nine members (originally seven) and that, except for procedural matters, the votes shall include 'the concurring votes of the [five] permanent members'. The one exception to this Charter rule is that in decisions relating to the pacific settlement of disputes, 'a party to a dispute shall abstain from voting' (Art. 27(3)). If nine or more of the 15 members vote in favour of a proposal, but one of the five permanent members votes 'no', the proposal is defeated. Until about 1970 the veto was used mainly by

TABLE 2.1   Vetoes in the Security Council, 1946–31
December 1993

	1946–55	1956–65	1966–75	1976–85	1986–93	Total
China	1	0	4	17	0	22
France	2	2	2	9	3	18
Soviet Union/ Russian Federation	77	26	11	7	2	123
UK	0	3	9	11	8	31
USA	0	0	12	37	21	70

the Soviet Union, but it has been increasingly resorted to by the three Western permanent members, especially the United States, usually on Middle Eastern or Southern African issues.

The use of the veto has significantly declined in recent years, with only one veto being exercised (by the Russian Federation) between 1990 and 1993. However, the potential of a veto being cast has come to act as a deterrent to controversial proposals even being brought before the Council.

Strictly speaking, an abstention should count as a veto, but the practice has been to regard an abstention as a concurring vote, so that only negative votes count as vetoes. Non-participation in the vote and absence are also regarded as forms of concurrence rather than vetoes.

The largest of the three UN Councils is that concerned with economic and social affairs – the Economic and Social Council, often abbreviated to ECOSOC, and not to be confused with UNESCO, the specialized agency of the United Nations concerned with education, science and culture.

ECOSOC has 54 members (originally 18), all elected by the General Assembly for a term of three years (Art. 61). The seats are distributed among the whole Membership of the United Nations on an equitable basis, although this is not required by the Charter. ECOSOC

has established a variety of regional and functional commissions and other bodies, and it is also empowered by
the Charter to 'co-ordinate the activities of the specialized agencies' (Art. 63(2)). ECOSOC considers general
policy questions regarding economic and social development, and makes recommendations (Art. 62).

One interesting feature of the Economic and Social
Council is that it is authorized by the Charter 'to make
suitable arrangements for consultation with non-governmental organisations' (NGOs) (Art. 71). Being itself concerned with international questions, ECOSOC has naturally
granted consultative status mainly to international rather
than national NGOs. Representatives of these bodies are
given facilities to follow the work of ECOSOC and its
subsidiary organs. They are entitled to receive documents,
have access to meetings, and may in certain circumstances
submit oral or written statements giving the experience
or views of their organization. Thus, religious representatives have made statements about religious liberty, trade
union representatives about forced labour, business representatives about international trade, and so on. It was
largely as a result of NGO pressure that the UN Commission on Human Rights (one of the subsidiary organs
of ECOSOC) decided in 1987 to recognize the right of
conscientious objection to military service.

There is clearly a role for non-governmental organizations so long as they do not try to usurp the functions of
governments. In a few matters, non-governmental bodies
have direct experience and knowledge which official bodies
cannot have. There are, for example, several non-governmental organizations with many years of first-hand experience of human rights or refugees, and this experience
can be useful to appropriate organs of the United Nations.

The third UN Council, the Trusteeship Council, has
two distinctive features of interest. First, it was decided
at San Francisco that membership of the Trusteeship
Council should be divided equally between states which
administer trust territories and states which do not (Art.
86). There would thus be a voting balance, so that neither

side would be able to force through the Council a decision unacceptable to the other. The non-colonial side of the Council was to consist of those of the five permanent members of the Security Council not administering trust territories (initially China and the Soviet Union), together with as many other members elected by the General Assembly as might be necessary to ensure that the Council would be equally divided.

It seems not to have been realized when the Charter was being drafted that the objectives of the trusteeship system would eventually be achieved, thus upsetting the voting balance on the Council. If an ordinary colonial power should cease to administer trust territories, it would lose its membership of the Trusteeship Council, thus displacing one elected member. If a power ceasing to administer trust territories should happen to be a permanent member of the Security Council, however, it would simply move to the other side, thus displacing two elected members.

The original system worked satisfactorily until 1960, when two trust territories in Africa which had previously been administered by France (Cameroons and Togoland) became independent. France continued as a member of the Trusteeship Council, but thereafter as a non-administering member. The non-colonial side now included a colonial power.

The situation became even more confused when Italy ceased to administer a trust territory later in 1960, Belgium and the UK in 1962, New Zealand in 1968, and Australia in 1975. This left the Council consisting of only one member from the colonial side (the United States, administering the Pacific Islands), the other four permanent members of the Security Council, and no members elected by the General Assembly.

The anti-colonial campaign of Third World and Communist countries had, in any case, been focused on two bodies not provided for in the Charter: a committee on information from non-self-governing territories and, from 1961, a committee 'to examine the application' of a Soviet-sponsored Declaration on decolonization.

The second interesting feature of the Trusteeship Council is that it is the only organ for which specific provision was made in the Charter for the receipt of petitions (Art. 87b). Individuals and organizations could petition the Council directly about conditions in trust territories, and in fact the volume of petitions and other communications was sometimes so great as to threaten to overwhelm the machinery of the United Nations. Although UN organs concerned with human rights had no authority under the Charter for receiving petitions, arrangements have been devised by these organs for considering 'communications' from aggrieved individuals or non-governmental agencies.

The General Assembly and the three Councils may set up subsidiary organs, especially for detailed studies between sessions of the parent body. Some organs set up for special purposes lapse when the work is completed; others are standing bodies and remain in being indefinitely. An example of a standing body is the Commission on Human Rights, which was set up by ECOSOC in 1946 and is still at work. A body with a short-term mandate was the Commission of Inquiry into the situation in the Seychelles, which was established by the Security Council on 15 December 1981 and which completed its mandate with a report dated 15 March 1982.

The Economic and Social Council and the Trusteeship Council operate 'under the authority of the General Assembly' (Arts. 60 and 85(2)), but the Assembly has no authority over the Security Council. The Security Council has primary responsibility for maintaining world peace and security (Art. 24(1)), and the Charter provides that while the Security Council is exercising the functions assigned to it in the Charter in respect of any dispute or situation, the General Assembly 'shall not make any recommendations with regard to that dispute or situation' (Art. 12(1)) and that the Assembly should refer to the Security Council 'any question on which action is necessary' (Art. 11(2)). It was apparently thought at San Francisco that these provisions would make it impossible for the two organs to deal concurrently with the same question.

In practice, however, the General Assembly has not been inclined to countenance any limit on its freedom to debate and recommend. For one thing, the Assembly may discuss a matter which is before the Security Council; the prohibitions are on the making of recommendations or taking action. Secondly, there is always room for argument about the precise meaning of the words 'While the Security Council is exercising . . . the functions assigned to it in the . . . Charter' or 'on which action is necessary'. It can be argued that the fact that a matter is on the list of items of which the Security Council is seized does not, of itself, constitute the exercise of functions, or that to make a request does not represent action. Indeed, the International Court of Justice considered that the kind of action referred to in Article 11(2) of the Charter is coercive or enforcement action. Finally, the Assembly has increasingly been able to take up a matter, or an aspect of a matter, with which the Security Council has been concerned, by claiming that what it is in fact considering is in some respects different from the matter before the Council.

The Assembly and the three Councils consist of states; the two other principal organs of the United Nations (the Secretariat and the International Court of Justice) are composed of individuals. The Secretariat comprises a Secretary-General appointed by the General Assembly on the recommendation of the Security Council (Art. 97), and other staff appointed by the Secretary-General (Art. 101). All staff members are supposed to act as international officials, responsible only to the United Nations, and should at all times be independent of all authorities external to the Organization (Art. 100). The paramount consideration in the employment of staff is said to be the necessity of securing the highest standards of performance and integrity, but due regard is also to be paid to the importance of recruiting on as wide a geographical basis as possible (Art. 101(3)).

The Secretariat services the policymaking organs (Arts. 98 and 101(2)), and the Secretary-General performs whatever other functions are entrusted to him by these organs (Art. 98). In addition, the Secretary-General has the right to 'bring to the attention of the Security Council' any matter which in his opinion may threaten world peace and security (Art. 99). This has provided successive Secretaries-General with a constitutional basis for a wide range of diplomatic and operational activities beyond those explicitly entrusted by the policy-making organs.

One of the most significant developments since the United Nations was founded has been the increasing tendency to entrust the Secretary-General and Secretariat with important responsibilities. To some extent this has reflected an enlarged conception of the functions which states regard it as proper for an international organization to undertake. But, in addition, there have been two other factors at work. First, the policymaking bodies have entrusted the Secretaries-General with important diplomatic and political tasks, although the mandates have often been expressed in broad general terms, allowing considerable latitude regarding interpretation and implementation: for example, 'Requests the Secretary-General to take any initiative that he deems helpful in relation to . . .'. Secondly, Secretaries-General have considered it within the letter and spirit of the Charter to take independent initiatives designed to safeguard world peace. Dissatisfaction within the Soviet bloc about Dag Hammarskjöld's initiatives and interpretations of Security Council resolutions regarding the Congo in 1960–61 led to the abortive troika proposal for tripartite administration.

Initial recruitment for the Secretariat was mainly from Western countries, and in 1946 83 per cent of the staff were Westerners. After the major admissions of UN Members in 1955 and 1960, pressure grew from Third World countries for a Secretariat recruited on a wider geographical basis, and the Communist states became more willing to release their nationals for short-term service with UN agencies. There has also been pressure to appoint more women to senior posts. A formula has been devised so that each UN Member has 'a desirable range' for the number of staff subject to geographical distribution: this range for the United Kingdom was 70 to 94 in 1993, with 83 UK citizens actually on the staff. Some countries are way beyond their desirable range. For the Philippines, for example, the range was from 4 to 14 in 1993, and the number in the Secretariat was 71.

The wider distribution of UN staff has been secured by substantially increasing the proportion of short-term staff, thus eroding the concept of an international career service. Staff seconded from national administrations tend to be careful not to offend their future employers while on loan to the United Nations. In a book published in 1962 one of us urged that a ceiling of 25 per cent be established for short-term staff. In the event, the proportion of short-term staff has more than doubled since 1956.

The idea of an impartial and non-partisan civil service is not universally accepted or understood. In many states the distinction between politics and administration is blurred. But the Charter is clear. Whatever views particular staff-members may hold in private, whatever the character of the government of the country of which they happen to be citizens, so long as they are employed in the United Nations Secretariat, their whole loyalty should be to the United Nations. If they cannot conscientiously take the oath or declaration of loyalty, they should not masquerade as international officials.

The other principal organ of the United Nations, the International Court of Justice, has its seat at the Hague. The Court consists of 15 independent judges elected regardless of nationality from among persons 'of high moral character' and who possess the highest judicial qualifications. The election should be conducted so that the main forms of civilization and the principal legal systems of the world are represented (Arts. 2–3 and 9 of the Statute). It is unnecessary to describe here the complicated procedures of nomination and election, except to say that the election of judges is a joint responsibility of the Security Council and the General Assembly, and that an absolute majority of votes is needed in both organs

– the only matter on which an absolute majority of votes in the Security Council suffices (originally six out of 11, now eight out of 15).

Only states may be parties to contentious cases before the Court. States are not under any obligation to submit cases for settlement, but they may decide to accept the compulsory jurisdiction of the Court, either unconditionally or on condition of reciprocity on the part of other states. Each member of the United Nations undertakes to comply with the decision of the Court in any case to which it is a party (Art. 94 of the Charter). The Court may, at the request of other United Nations organs, give advisory opinions on legal questions.

The Court is in permanent session, except for judicial vacations, and may sit at the Hague or elsewhere as needed. It elects its own President and Vice-President, and appoints a Registrar and other officers. Decisions of the Court are taken in private by majority vote, the quorum being nine. The judgement of the Court must state the reasons on which it is based.

One other important feature of the UN system is not mentioned in the Charter: the permanent diplomatic missions of the Members. It was originally expected that all UN organs would meet at predictable times, except for the Security Council, which was to be 'so organized as to be able to function continuously' (Art. 28(1)). That meant that 11 out of the original 51 Members of the United Nations had to maintain permanent staffs at UN Headquarters. In the course of time, as the number of UN organs increased, as sessions of UN bodies took longer, and as inter-sessional subsidiary organs were created, more and more countries established permanent missions at UN Headquarters. Most UN Members now have permanent missions in New York, though in some cases the ambassador is also accredited to the US Government in Washington.

These permanent missions are much like ordinary embassies or legations, but three important differences should be noted. First, although the Permanent Representatives of Members of the United Nations present credentials to the Secretary-General, they are not accredited to the Secretary-General in the way that an ambassador is accredited to the head of state of the country in which he or she serves. There is, moreover, no requirement that the Secretary-General should give prior approval to the appointment of a particular person. Secondly, the permanent mission of a UN Member has responsibilities regarding the United Nations but not for relations with the host-country; these are handled separately in Washington rather than in New York. Thirdly, persons on the staff of national missions to the United Nations need qualifications additional to those normally expected of foreign service officers. UN delegates are, in a sense, accredited to more than 180 countries rather than to just one; with some of these his or her own nation may not have diplomatic relations. UN delegates must learn the formal and informal procedures of UN organs and be able to take tactical advantage of unexpected situations; they must establish civilized personal relations with a variety of foreigners, some of whom they may find disagreeable; they must be able to handle representatives of the press; and they must be able to speak clearly and convincingly in public at short notice. Gladwyn Jebb, the British ambassador at the United Nations from 1950 to 1954, gained a considerable reputation in the United States for his effective speeches in the Security Council on the Korean question.

The organization and structure described in this chapter derive, in the main, from the Charter. To amend the Charter there must be a favourable vote of two-thirds of the Members of the United Nations, including all five permanent members of the Security Council. But the fact that the United Nations Charter cannot easily be amended has not prevented adjustment of practice within the Charter's general framework. In at least two instances, indeed, there has been a tacit agreement that the words of the Charter shall be interpreted in a way quite different from their apparent meaning. First, the article of the Charter dealing with voting in the Security Council

TABLE 2.2 Composition of the five principal organs

Organ	Composition	Method of election or appointment	Charter
General Assembly	All Members of the United Nations	–	Art. 9(1)
Security Council	(1) Five permanent members Republic of China, France, Soviet Union/Russian Federation, United Kingdom, and United States of America	–	Art. 23(1)
	(2) Ten (originally six) non-permanent members for two-year terms	Election by General Assembly, due regard being specially paid in the first instance to the contribution of Members to the maintenance of international peace and security and other purposes of the United Nations, and also to equitable geographical distribution. Since 1965 there has been a geographical formula for distribution of elective seats.	Art. 23(11)
Economic and Social Council	Originally 18 members increased to 27 in 1965 and to 54 in 1973.	Election by General Assembly, with a geographical pattern for elections since 1971.	Art. 61

continued on page 32

TABLE 2.2 continued

Organ	Composition	Method of election or appointment	Charter
Secretariat			
(1) Secretary-General	–	Appointment by General Assembly upon recommendation of Security Council.	Art. 97
(2) Other staff	–	Appointment by Secretary-General under regulations established by General Assembly. The paramount consideration in employment of staff shall be the necessity of securing the highest standards of efficiency, competence and integrity. Due regard shall be paid to the importance of recruiting staff on as wide a geographical basis as possible.	Art. 101(1) and (3)
International Court of Justice	15 independent judges	Election by General Assembly and Security Council for nine-year terms. The Court shall be composed of judges elected regardless of nationality from among persons of high moral character, and who have the highest judicial qualifications. The persons elected should individually possess the qualifications required; and the Court as a whole should include representatives of the main forms of civilization and of the principal legal systems of the world.	Statute Arts. 2–3, 8–9

states that decisions on non-procedural matters shall include 'the concurring votes of the [five] permanent members'. The man or woman in the street would not regard this statement as ambiguous: it means, or appears to mean, that one of the permanent members of the Council can block a decision simply by failing to vote 'yes'. A negative vote, or an abstention, or non-participation in the vote, or absence from the Council: any of these methods, it might be thought, could be used to prevent a decision. But, in practice, only a negative vote by a permanent member has been regarded as a veto, and an abstention or non-participation in the vote or absence is regarded as a form of concurrence. There has been no formal proposal to amend the Charter, and the World Court has described the present procedure as 'a general practice' which has been 'generally accepted'. The second example of a *de facto* change without formal Charter amendment is that since 24 December 1991, the references in the Charter to the Union of Soviet Socialist Republics have been replaced by 'the Russian Federation'.

The Charter is not perfect, but it is the only Charter we have. The challenge is not to devise a constitution for some future utopia but to make the best use of the Charter we have in this present, imperfect world.

3 Groups and Blocs

Some of the more optimistic speeches at San Francisco in 1945 seemed to suggest that the United Nations, simply by existing, would put an end to all international conflict. While it is legitimate to hope for the best, it is only realistic to assume that disputes between nations and between groups of nations will continue to disturb world peace. The leaders of most countries believe that such disputes are inevitable, so they arm accordingly, in the hope that military capabilities backed by resolute leadership will deter war.

Moreover, there were optimists at San Francisco who hoped that the system of collective security laid down in the Charter would make military alliances unnecessary. It is true that the Charter does not impair the inherent right of 'individual or collective self-defence if an armed attack occurs' (Art. 51) and that 'regional arrangements or agencies' are permitted so long as they are consistent with the principles and purposes of the United Nations (Arts. 52–4); but these provisions were not to vitiate the primary responsibility of the Security Council for dealing with international disputes or threatening situations, and the Security Council was to be informed of measures taken in exercise of the right of self-defence and of similar 'activities undertaken or in contemplation' on a regional basis (Arts. 51, 54). The fact that the Charter made express provision for regional arrangements seems to have been due in part to Winston Churchill's enthusiasm during the Second World War for a United Nations based on strong regional groupings.

The plan for collective measures by the United Nations in the event of threats to or breaches of the peace or acts of aggression has never been properly implemented, because of disagreement about the national forces which were to be placed at the disposal of the Security Council.

In the absence of a reliable United Nations system of collective security, states have sought security in neutrality or non-alignment or in military alliances.

Much may be said about alliances of this kind, but we want to stress four points here. First, they were created in the belief that the UN system was inadequate to ensure the security of the Members. Secondly, existing military alliances have in practice not conformed to all the requirements of the Charter, for the Security Council is not regularly or consistently informed of measures taken or contemplated on a self-defence or regional basis. Thirdly, all Members of the United Nations have expressly agreed that their obligations under the UN Charter prevail over their obligations under other international agreements (Art. 103). Fourthly, and most important, limited alliances tend to induce habits of thought and vested military, political and commercial interests inimical to the development in the future of a sound system of collective security on a universal basis. Although such a goal may now seem far beyond our reach, we should recognize that some of the steps now being taken in the hope of preserving peace in the short run may make the long-term goal seem even more utopian than would otherwise be the case.

If the United Nations cannot at present provide a guaranteed system of collective security, it can at least seek to soften the sharp edges of controversy and conflict. And here we encounter a paradox, for the processes which have evolved in the United Nations often have contrary effects. On the one hand, the informal aspects of parliamentary diplomacy can most certainly help to remove misunderstanding and foster agreement. There is constant discussion and negotiation in the lobbies and lounges. Representatives of more than 180 countries meet casually or by arrangement almost every day of the year at UN Headquarters in New York – they relax in the same lounge, eat in the same dining-room, drink at the same bar, patronize the same hairdresser. Many of these men and women acquire a professional pride in the United

Nations as an institution, a sense of solidarity and common purpose. We do not wish to exaggerate either the extent or the effects of the personal understanding which develops across political barriers, but it undoubtedly facilitates the conduct of diplomacy in the modern world. A negative side of the coin is that parliamentary diplomacy constantly forces countries to take sides. It is usually taken for granted that UN debate (except for the Security Council) is merely a prelude to a vote; it is often said by parties to conflict that other countries have a duty to stand up and be counted. Three times out of four, to be sure, a vote may be necessary: it would be impossible to conduct the business of the United Nations without voting. All the same, issues have often been brought to an unnecessary or premature vote, thereby exacerbating rather than relieving the tension. There is a sense in which for many years the only vote on apartheid that really mattered was the vote of South Africa.

The fact that a quasi-parliamentary process is at work in the United Nations fosters some of the manifestations which we tend to associate with an ordinary party system – caucuses, whips, slates of candidates, lobbying, horse-trading, log-rolling, and so on. Some of this diplomatic manoeuvring takes place in the various capitals, but it is mainly centred in New York, and to a lesser extent in Geneva and other UN bases. Just as political parties within a nation emerged when individuals put aside differences of detail in order to act unitedly for larger ends, so nations associate in pursuit of their common regional or ideological interests.

In order to facilitate the working of multilateral diplomacy, the UN building in New York was designed to be more than simply a series of conference rooms and offices. UN Headquarters include lounges and lobbies, dining-rooms and snack bars, a library, a post office, a medical clinic, a bank, a travel agency, a bookshop, a hairdresser, a meditation room. The United Nations, being on international territory, employs its own uniformed guards.

On most days of the year, meetings of UN organs take place. In addition to the delegates participating in these meetings, other delegates will be present as observers, or to meet colleagues by arrangement, or perhaps just to judge the mood at the United Nations. There will also be journalists and representatives of non-governmental organizations. Groups huddle in the delegates' lounge or in quiet corners of the building, and the experienced diplomat or journalist will speculate as to why the ambassador of Afghanistan, say, is talking so earnestly to the ambassador of Zimbabwe, or whether the absence of delegates from a particular regional group means that a caucus is being held. Some observers will make deductions from the announcements in a variety of languages over the public address system in the delegates' lounge, speculating why Madame Albino is waiting by the switchboard to meet ambassador Zimmertal, or whether the unexpectedly early closing of the meeting in conference room 18 means that an obstacle has been encountered or an agreement has been reached or simply that the committee has run out of speakers. Diplomats are on the *qui vive* for the loudspeakers to announce emergency meetings of regional or ideological groups, bodies which have no official status at the United Nations but are now a necessary part of the international diplomatic process.

The regional groups at the United Nations have existed from the very beginning, but a formal recognition of their existence dates from the decision in 1963 about the distribution of elective seats into four regions: Africa and Asia, Eastern Europe, Latin America, 'Western Europe and other States'. In 1971, the daily *UN Journal* began publishing the names of the Chairmen of regional groups for the month, but separating Africa from Asia. Over a period of time, it is possible to deduce the membership of the five regions from the elections to those UN bodies with an agreed formula for geographical distribution and the monthly information in the *Journal* about chairmanship. There are sub-groups in all the regions.

It would be convenient if groups of states at the United

Nations corresponded exactly to geographical regions. This would greatly simplify the application of the Charter requirement that among the criteria for electing states to the Security Council should be 'equitable geographical distribution' (Art. 23(i)), or the appointment of staff 'on as wide a geographical basis as possible' (Art. 101(3)). The problem of implementing these provisions would be easier to deal with if the states in each region were sufficiently homogeneous that any one of them could be regarded as broadly representative of the region as a whole. But there are differences within every region.

Consider the Middle East. The region is thought of by many as inhabited entirely by people who speak Arabic and are Muslim by religion. It is, indeed, true that the core of the region is so composed, but the region also includes Lebanon (in which the population is Arabic-speaking but almost equally divided between Christians and Muslims), Egypt (Arabic-speaking and mainly Muslim, but with a minority of Christian Copts), two states whose people are mainly Muslim but who do not speak Arabic (Iran and Turkey), Israel (mainly Jewish but with a minority of Muslim or Christian Palestinian Arabs), and Cyprus which, until 1974, had a Greek-speaking and Orthodox Christian majority but which included a Muslim minority most of whom were Turkish-speaking.

It has sometimes been urged that the Middle East is such an important region that it should always have one representative on the Security Council: but it is one thing to demand this in theory and quite another thing to apply it in practice. Which state can properly 'represent' the Middle East?

This diversity within regions is not just a matter for discussion in lecture-rooms or books. The great powers reached an informal understanding in 1946 about the distribution of the members to be elected by the General Assembly to the Security Council. Part of this understanding was that one of the six should be an East European state – although there has been disagreement as to whether the understanding was to apply only to the 1946 elections or was to have ongoing validity. At any rate, Poland was elected for 1946–47 and the Ukraine for 1948–49, thus maintaining the 1946 understanding in full. For the period 1950–51, and again for 1956, the General Assembly elected for Eastern Europe Yugoslavia, a Communist state which had broken with the Soviet bloc; Greece was elected to fill the vacancy for 1952–53 and Turkey for 1954–55. The so-called East European seat was filled by the Philippines in 1957 and by Japan in 1958–59. Poland split the 1960–61 term with Liberia, Romania the 1962–63 term with the Philippines, and Czechoslovakia the 1964–65 term with Malaysia. The Security Council was then enlarged from 11 to 15 members, and one of the elective seats was firmly allocated to Eastern Europe for the future.

The Soviet Union had contended that, apart from the years when there had been no pretence of filling the seat by a state from Eastern Europe (1957, 1959, 1963, and 1965), the election of countries outside the Soviet bloc to 'represent' Eastern Europe was a breach of the spirit if not the letter of the 1946 understanding. The Soviet Union favoured a system analogous to the primary elections in the United States, in which candidates would be selected by the countries of the region concerned. This view has gained increasing support in other regions.

There are anomalies in all regions. Israel and South Africa, though from the Afro-Asian geographical region, did not attend meetings of the Afro-Asian group. Cuba, a Latin American state, was for a time excluded from meetings of the Latin American group. Turkey is both Middle Eastern and European. It is a member of the Afro-Asian group, and chairs the Asian regional group about once every two years. It is also a signatory of the North Atlantic Treaty and regularly chairs the 'West European and other States' group. Moreover, Turkey occupied the East European seat on the Security Council in 1951–52, 1954–55, and 1961. Turkey has somehow managed to belong to three regional groups simultaneously.

All of the informal regional associations of states at

United Nations Headquarters call themselves 'groups' – a conveniently non-committal word. Until the collapse of the Soviet Union and the dissolution of the Warsaw Pact, the countries associated with the Soviet Union were formally called a 'bloc'. This difference of terminology was useful, because the Soviet bloc did differ from the other groups. It was usually more disciplined than regional groups, and had greater cohesion. It had a recognized leader – the Soviet Union. It shared a common ideology – Marxism. The bloc's European members were military allies in the Warsaw Pact and members of COMECON. The Soviet bloc countries cooperated closely at both the governmental and the party level.

Members of the Soviet bloc usually adopted the same public position on important international questions. It is true that there were a few occasions on which members of the bloc voted differently in UN organs, but such deviations were rare. There were sometimes interesting differences in the tone of voice or choice of language of Soviet bloc speakers, but these differences of emphasis did not alter the fact that the countries of the Soviet bloc tried to present a united front on international issues in public.

The Soviet Union, as the first country to undergo a Marxist revolution, a country of considerable material power and a permanent member of the Security Council, enjoyed a position of special pre-eminence and leadership within the bloc. The countries of the Soviet camp believed that, having embarked on the Marxist road, they had minimized (if not eliminated) internal contradictions, so that important differences of foreign policy were inconceivable. For the first four decades after the Second World War, the Soviet bloc faced a loose pro-Western coalition, usually comprising the military allies of the United States, the European neutrals, most Latin American countries, Nationalist China, and Israel. For some UN elections the Western countries came under the heading 'Western Europe and other States'. This category was and is rather ambiguous, because 'Western Europe' really meant non-Communist Europe, and it was not always clear which were the 'other States': from the elections to the two UN Councils since they were enlarged in 1965, it would seem that Canada, Australia, and New Zealand are among the 'other' states.

It was sometimes said in the early days that the United States had an 'automatic majority' at the United Nations; but no UN vote is ever 'automatic'. What *was* true was that the United States could nearly always organize a sufficient vote to prevent any other coalition from gaining the two-thirds majority needed for important questions in the General Assembly (Art. 18(2)).

Within the original pro-Western coalition was one regional group which has met regularly as a caucus since the United Nations was founded, especially to select candidates for elective office. Among the 51 original Members of the United Nations were 20 Latin American republics, bound together by tradition, culture and religion. All these countries were originally colonized from the Mediterranean area: the Roman Catholic religion predominates; all, except Brazil and Haiti, are Spanish-speaking; all, along with the United States, have belonged to the Organization of American States. As the Membership of the United Nations increased, the relative strength of the Latin American group declined, until it was invigorated by the admission of 13 former colonies in the Caribbean area.

The Latin American and Caribbean group at the UN normally meets about once a week while the General Assembly is in session, and about once a month at other times of the year. Voting at meetings of the group is infrequent. The Latin American countries usually supported the United States on Cold War issues in the early days, but the region has become increasingly diverse since 1959, when Fidel Castro gained power in Cuba. All the states of the region are anti-colonial, and in some cases they are relatively underdeveloped. While they are not technically neutral, since they have mutual defence arrangements, some of them have been associated with the non-aligned movement and have sought to exert a moderating influence in UN affairs. Cuba was a member of COMECON, and some Latin American or Caribbean states participated in the conference of non-aligned countries in May 1993.

As decolonization proceeded and formerly dependent territories exercised self-determination and achieved UN Membership, the centre of gravity in the United Nations began to shift. By 1961 the Afro-Asian countries could command a simple majority of votes in the General Assembly, and a two-thirds vote if they could gain the support of either the Soviet bloc or a majority of Latin American or Western countries.

The largest UN groups comprise both the 52 African states (of which ten are Arab) and the 45 Asian and Pacific states (of which 12 are Arab). The Afro-Asian group drew much of its initial inspiration from the Bandung Conference of 1955, in which China played a prominent part, though for some years earlier, an informal group of Asian and African countries, fluctuating in composition, had been meeting at UN Headquarters for limited purposes. The countries of the Afro-Asian group possess less military or economic power than their developed counterparts. The core of most of their economies is subsistence agriculture; their export trade may be confined to a single product; educational and medical services are often minimal. In some of them, indeed, even the structure of the state is rudimentary. But these countries, conscious of their material weakness, find in the United Nations a forum in which weakness is not a major disadvantage. The Afro-Asian group was thus the international mouthpiece of the revolution of rising expectations. The group is by no means always in agreement but, as a generalization, it may be said that they have stood for the rapid liquidation of the vestiges of colonialism and racism, support for the Palestinian Arabs, a large-scale programme of multilateral aid to the less-developed parts of the world, and non-alignment during the Cold War era. The group meets regularly at the United Nations, the chairmanship rotating.

Efforts are made to reach a consensus without voting.

Within the Afro-Asian group are a number of sub-alignments. The most significant of these is the Arab group of 22 states. Major questions of direct concern to the Arab countries are considered by the Council of the Arab League, which meets from time to time in one of the Arab countries. The Arab League has an office in New York which coordinates the Arab approach to UN issues. The Arab group at the United Nations normally meets at least once a month. The group includes countries with revolutionary governments (Libya) as well as more conservative monarchies (Saudi Arabia), but one political issue unites them: support for the Palestinian Arabs and varying degrees of hostility to Israel. Arabs regard the Israeli Jews as intruders who have stolen Palestinian land and ousted Palestinian people. In 1948 the Arabs took up arms against Israel, and there were wars between Israel and Arab states in 1956, 1967 and 1973. One subgroup of Arab states in Asia is the Gulf Cooperation Council (six members), and an Asian sub-group is the Association of South-East Asian Nations (ASEAN) (five members).

There were originally two groupings of African countries, but these merged in 1963 to form the Organization of African Unity. The African nations constitute the largest UN coalition, with as many members as the founder Members of the United Nations itself. It was not unknown for their foreign ministers to congregate in New York for a UN debate on apartheid or Namibia during a period when an African diplomat was presiding over the Security Council. On one famous occasion in 1966 the Security Council was prevented from meeting for more than 48 hours because the African state whose turn it was to preside was unwilling to convene the Council until the African group had coordinated its stance on Southern Rhodesia.

Most of the Afro-Asian countries attend meetings of the nonaligned states, the summit meetings of which are now usually attended by about a hundred states. The Group of 77 was originally formed at a meeting of the UN Con-

TABLE 3.1 Geographical distribution of UN Membership,
1 January 1994

Africa: Members of the Organization of African Unity, of which ten are members of the Arab League, plus South Africa	53
Asia: Asian group, of which 12 are members of the Arab League, plus Israel	44
Eastern Europe	27*
Latin America: 18 Spanish-speaking, one Portuguese-speaking (Brazil), one French-speaking (Haiti), plus 12 former British colonies, and one former Netherlands colony (Surinam)	33
Western Europe and Other States:	
Western Europe 23	
Older Commonwealth (Australia, Canada, New Zealand) 3	27
United States 1	
	184

* This figure includes the constituent republics of the former Soviet Union. It also includes Serbia-Montenegro (former Yugoslavia) whose participation in certain UN activities was suspended as we went to press.

ference on Trade and Development (UNCTAD) to coordinate the Third World approach to development issues.

Perhaps the most unusual group of all is the Commonwealth, since it has neither geographical nor ideological unity. The 46 Commonwealth members of the UN are shown in Table 3.2.

The Commonwealth was once described to one of us in the following terms: 'The Commonwealth cannot be defined, but it undoubtedly exists. We meet from time to time to exchange views on matters on which we are agreed. We always vote for each other, unless we happen to prefer some other candidate. It is a very superior form of cooperation but it cannot be copied.'

The Commonwealth group meets infrequently. Proceedings are informal, and there is no voting. In the early

TABLE 3.2   Commonwealth Members of the UN

Europe	Africa	Asia	Oceania*	The Americas
Cyprus	Botswana	Bangladesh	Australia	Antigua and
Malta	Gambia	Brunei	New Zealand	Barbuda
United	Ghana	Darussalam	Papua New	Bahamas
Kingdom	Kenya	India	Guinea	Barbados
	Lesotho	Malaysia	Samoa	Belize
	Malawi	Maldives	Solomon	Canada
	Mauritius	Pakistan	Islands	Dominica
	Namibia	Singapore	Vanuatu	Grenada
	Nigeria	Sri Lanka		Guyana
	Seychelles			Jamaica
	Sierra Leone			St Kitts and
	Swaziland			Nevis
	Tanzania			St Lucia
	Uganda			St Vincent
	Zambia			and the
	Zimbabwe			Grenadines
				Trinidad and
				Tobago

* Fiji's membership of the Commonwealth was deemed to have lapsed with the emergence of the Republic on 15 October 1987.

days, Commonwealth countries usually agreed on candidates for Commonwealth seats on UN organs.

The dynamic nature of international politics inevitably leads to changes in the composition and outlook of some of the groups. A local dispute within a region may be followed by differences on wider issues. All the regional groups have tended to become more diverse, so that alignments are often in a fluid state. Internal differences within a group may manifest themselves in split votes in the General Assembly, but without actually leading to changes of alignment.

Bloc voting is, perhaps, most interesting where it is least visible – that is to say, in secret balloting. All elections by the General Assembly are by secret ballot, and there are supposed to be no nominations. When the General Assembly comes to elect members of the two Councils or those of its own officers elected by the plenary, there is theoretically an unfettered choice. There is, to be sure, nearly always a general understanding about the distribution or rotation of certain seats, but this cannot prevent two or more candidates from offering themselves for a particular vacancy. In 1993 the UK and Sweden were both candidates for the Advisory Committee on Administrative and Budgetary Questions (ACABQ) but Sweden garnered more votes and thus displaced the UK – the first time that a Permanent Member of the Security Council had lost its seat on this important body. Furthermore, the competition is complicated by the requirement of the Charter that a two-thirds majority is needed in some elections. This means that a minority of UN Members (one-third plus one) can compel the Assembly to continue balloting indefinitely.

4 Peace and Security

The UN organ with primary responsibility for maintaining peace and security is the Security Council (Article 24 of the Charter). This Council has varying degrees of coercive power. It can place a matter on its agenda, debate the issue, conduct an investigation, recommend procedures or terms of settlement or other provisional measures. The Council may also authorize peace-keeping, for which there is no express provision in the Charter, but Dag Hammarskjöld once called it Chapter Six-and-a-half. Peace-keeping operations have been especially appropriate for policing demilitarized zones, disputed frontiers, or for maintaining law and order in areas of tension. A more coercive procedure, for which the Charter expressly provides, requires measures not involving military action, often known in UN circles as sanctions (Art. 41). 'These may include complete or partial interruption of economic relations and of rail, sea, air, postal, telegraphic, radio, and other means of communication, and the severance of diplomatic relations.' If such measures would be or have proved to be inadequate, the Security Council may take such military action as may be necessary (Art. 42).

Peacemaking, in UN jargon, refers to a procedure for the peaceful settlement of an international dispute. In some recent contexts, it has been used to refer to peace-enforcement undertaken through the authority of Chapter VII of the UN Charter. There is sometimes a difference of opinion in UN organs as to whether a dispute is international or domestic, and borderline cases are often admitted to the agenda of UN organs on the ground that the issues, although internal in origin, have become a potential if not an actual threat to world peace. That argument carried weight when the Security Council decided in 1960 to act against apartheid in South Africa.

States which join the United Nations undertake to settle

their international disputes by peaceful means (Art. 2(3)), and the Security Council is empowered to call on the parties to a dispute to settle it peacefully (Art. 33(2)) or the Council may go further and recommend 'appropriate procedures or methods of adjustment' or actual 'terms of settlement' (Arts. 36(1) and 37(2)). The Charter contains an illustrative list of peaceful means which the parties may use 'first of all': negotiation, inquiry, mediation, conciliation, arbitration, judicial settlement, resort to regional agencies or arrangements – to which the Charter, to be on the safe side, adds 'or other peaceful means of their own choice' (Art. 33(1)). One of the means not listed in the Charter is the provision of good offices, which is akin to mediation and conciliation.

Several Articles of the Charter refer to a dispute or situation (for example, Arts. 14, 34, 35(1) and 36(1)). The drafters of the Charter seem to have given little thought to the difference between the two, but in practice states have become increasingly hesitant to claim that a complaint against another state constitutes a dispute, because of the Charter requirement that the parties to a dispute 'shall abstain from voting' on proposals for a peaceful settlement in the Security Council. To avoid losing voting support, a state with a grievance is likely to complain that there is merely a situation which is likely to endanger international peace and security.

In order to determine whether a situation or dispute is likely to escalate, and before offering third-party assistance in achieving a settlement, the Security Council may decide on an investigation (Art. 34). The General Assembly has also authorized various kinds of investigation or observation, acting within its wide general powers under the Charter to discuss and recommend (Arts. 10–12) or under its specific power to initiate studies (Art. 13(1)). UN missions of investigation may be initiated by the Security Council, the General Assembly or the Secretary-General.

The scope of such operations has been considerable; examples from the 1940s included the Truce Supervision

Organization in the Middle East (UNTSO) and the Military Observer Group in India and Pakistan (UNMOGIP). The 1950s and 1960s witnessed a growth in UN observer missions ranging from the UN Observer Group in the Lebanon (UNOGIL) to the UN Yemen Observation Mission (UNYOM). The 1970s saw the development of UN peace-keeping with the UN Disengagement Force (UNDOF) in the Golan Heights and the UN Interim Force in Lebanon (UNIFIL). The 1980s and early 1990s have also seen a plethora of similar missions, ranging from specialists to investigate allegations of the use of chemical weapons in the Iraq–Iran war (1984 and 1986) to the UN Observer Mission in Liberia (UNOMIL) in 1993.

The Charter refers repeatedly to the 'settlement' of disputes, but many disputes are not 'settled' in any ultimate sense. Cyprus and Kashmir have been before the Security Council for more than 30 years. The world is having to learn to live with a host of unsatisfied grievances and unresolved problems.

The United Nations is not a substitute for traditional diplomacy: indeed, resort to the United Nations is often thought of as an act of diplomatic warfare rather than a means of solving a problem. States go to the UN to let off steam, to air grievances, to embarrass adversaries, to engage in ideological polemics, to advocate utopian but unrealizable goals. This is time-consuming and disagreeable for diplomats with more constructive purposes in mind, but 'jaw-jaw is better than war-war' (Winston Churchill, 26 June 1954).

Let us look at some of the procedures or methods of adjustment which are available to parties who genuinely want a settlement. Negotiation is *par excellence* the method to be used first of all, for it involves only the parties: all the other means of settlement require the assistance of a third party (Art. 33(i)).

Inquiry is a procedure for establishing the facts in order to facilitate a settlement. Inquiry should be distinguished from investigation which, in the UN, is a procedure open to the Security Council 'to determine whether the continuance of the dispute or situation is likely to endanger the maintenance of international peace and security' (Art. 34). Inquiry is to assist the parties, investigation to assist the Security Council.

Mediation and conciliation are mentioned in the Charter, good offices is not. All involve third-party assistance in identifying and elucidating the issues, without necessarily recommending terms of settlement. An attempt is usually made to keep the proceedings as informal as possible. The main tangible weapon at the disposal of the third party providing assistance is the threat to publish a report, if necessary identifying the party which has proved most recalcitrant.

The intermediary for mediation, conciliation, or good offices may be an individual or a committee appointed by an organ of the United Nations or of a regional agency, as was the case with Count Bernadotte for the UN in the Middle East in 1948, and with Lord Owen for the EC/EU following the break-up of Yugoslavia.The intermediary may also be an appointee of a single government, as was the role of Norway regarding the Israeli–Palestine problem in 1993, so long as he or she is acceptable to the parties. Occasionally the intermediary is a private individual from a humanitarian agency who is trusted by both sides; this is sometimes called Track Two Diplomacy.We have both had experience of this role, which requires the capacity to listen patiently to what is being said, even if you have heard it many times before, and the ability to detect in what you hear those occasional nuggets which represent a more conciliatory stance than the other side will have realized from public pronouncements.

The aim of arbitration is to produce a judgment, usually called an award, which is binding on the parties.

The next procedure for peaceful settlement is resort to a judicial tribunal. There have always been people who have regarded international law as the heart of the problem of international relations. They point out that the progressive achievement of order and peace within states has been accompanied by increasing respect for law and legal institutions. But law in our day is often overshadowed by politics. Many leaders of the newer countries of Asia and Africa are distrustful of aspects of international law which evolved in the West.

Two UN organs are exclusively concerned with international law. The International Court of Justice, with its seat at the Hague, is one of the principal organs of the United Nations (Art. 7(1)). It decides those disputes between states which are submitted to it, and gives advisory opinions on legal questions. The International Law Commission, a subsidiary organ of the General Assembly, has no responsibility for adjudication but is charged with promoting the progressive development and codification of international law (Art. 13(1)a).

All members of the United Nations are automatically parties to the Statute of the International Court of Justice (Art. 93(1)), and two states which do not belong to the United Nations have become parties (see Appendix 3(a)). A state may opt to accept the compulsory jurisdiction of the Court, either unconditionally or with conditions such as reciprocity or restricted duration, but only 56 of the 186 parties to the Statute have exercised this option.

The Charter states that legal disputes should 'as a general rule' be referred by the parties to the International Court of Justice (Art. 36(3)) or a similar tribunal (Art. 95). UN Members have undertaken to comply with the Court's decisions in any cases to which they are parties (Art. 94(1)), though this undertaking has not been observed in all cases. Following the mining of British warships in Albanian waters in 1946, the United Kingdom and Albania agreed to submit the case to the Hague Court. The Court found that the UK had not violated Albanian sovereignty by sending ships through the Strait, but that the subsequent minesweeping operation was such a violation. The Court found that compensation of £843 947 was due to the UK, but Albania has declined to pay. Forty years later, Nicaragua instituted proceedings against the United States because of alleged US responsibility for laying mines in Nicaraguan waters and other hostile military action. The United States withdrew its acceptance of the compulsory jurisdiction of the Court, and also withdrew from the case on a technicality. On most of the substantive issues, the Court found that the United States had violated international law. The Court has the power under its Statute (Art. 41) to order provisional measures to preserve the rights of either party, as it did in 1993 when Bosnia-Herzegovina alleged that Serbia and Montenegro were engaging in acts of genocide. The Court may also give an advisory opinion, as it did in 1971 in response to a request from the General Assembly for advice regarding the status of South-West Africa (Namibia).

The International Court has given some important decisions and advisory opinions. Unlike national courts, the International Court cannot exercise jurisdiction unless the parties agree; the direction in which to move is to extend the area of compulsory jurisdiction. There is, in almost every international dispute, some element susceptible of judicial solution.

The other legal organ of the United Nations, the International Law Commission, has made a little progress in codifying international law; that is to say, in drafting international instruments on subjects on which there is already a fair measure of agreement. It has hardly come to grips yet with its other task of *developing* international law.

If this were a book about the United Nations as we would like the Organization to be rather than about the United Nations as it is, we would give more attention to judicial methods of dealing with the legal aspects of international disputes. If nations are to live in peace, their relations must to some extent be governed by legal rules and principles. It has to be admitted, however, that international law is at present primitive. It is largely uncodified, and the means for enforcing international legal decisions are inadequate.

Regional agencies or arrangements are said in the

Charter to be especially appropriate for the pacific settlement of local disputes (Art. 52(2)). The inclusion of regional means of settlement in the Charter's illustrative list has in practice been used not to settle a dispute but to prevent UN organs from taking up an issue, on the ground that it was being or should be dealt with on a regional basis. This argument was used in 1954 over a Guatemalan complaint of aggression, in 1958 over a Lebanese complaint of intervention in its domestic affairs by the United Arab Republic, in 1965 after US troops had landed in the Dominican Republic, and again over Nicaraguan complaints against the United States after 1982.

When regional organizations *have* been utilised, they have seldom had the infrastructure, resources, or experience to engage successfully in conflict-resolution. The difficulty of demarcating lines of responsibility between the UN and OAS in the Dominican Republic in 1965, and the ineffective role of the Organization of African Unity in Chad in 1981 point to the difficulties entailed in utilizing regional organizations. The Conference on Security and Cooperation in Europe (CSCE) and European Community attempts to tackle the Balkans conflict following the break-up of Yugoslavia similarly point to the problems encountered in attempting a division of labour between a regional organization and the UN. The UN, however, has cooperated effectively with regional organizations in monitoring elections.

Means of settlement are the procedures aimed at a specific solution: *terms* of settlement are the actual proposals or agreements which are designed to bring a conflict to an end (Art. 37(2)). In the early days, the Security Council drew up detailed terms of settlement in a number of cases. This was done over Kashmir (21 April 1948), for example, and Indonesia (28 January 1949). The snag about this method was that if the situation subsequently changed, as soon happened in the Indonesian case, the Security Council found itself committed to terms which had been overtaken by events. After the adoption of the Indonesian resolution but before the UN Committee of

Good Offices on the spot could get down to implementing it, the Indonesian nationalists and the Dutch government agreed to hold a round table conference in the Hague. The Security Council had to resort to a rather unsatisfactory procedural gimmick so as to disengage from its earlier decision.

If the Council is not to recommend terms of settlement, it can at least decide which means or procedures of settlement would be appropriate in a particular case (Art. 36(1)). Selecting an example, in the Middle East, the mediating function was initially entrusted to a single individual (Count Folke Bernadotte of Sweden, then Ralph Bunche after Bernadotte's assassination) but, the following year, Bunche recommended to the Security Council that the function of promoting a peaceful settlement should be transferred to the three-state Palestine Conciliation Commission. No sooner had the Council acted on the advice that mediation should be entrusted to a commission rather than a single individual than it received the opposite advice from another source!

In the first phase in Kashmir, the intermediary function had been entrusted to a commission of five states. The Security Council was no doubt bemused when the commission reported in 1949 that a five-member body was not flexible enough, and that a single mediator with broad authority and undivided responsibility would offer a more practical means of finding a compromise.

The truth is that neither a single intermediary nor a collective body has decisive advantages over the other. When one method has exhausted its utility, nothing is lost by trying another method.

One difficulty about collective bodies for mediation is that, if they are established on an equitable regional basis, the members may have to spend more time negotiating with each other than solving the problem.

Even in connection with a single issue, a variety of methods of third-party assistance may be used, as is shown by the range of methods tried in connection with the Palestine question. In 1948, Count Bernadotte was appointed 'Mediator in Palestine' and he was also asked to 'use his good offices' for several purposes, including the promotion of 'a peaceful adjustment of the future situation in Palestine'. In 1951, the Security Council asked the Chief of Staff of the UN Truce Supervision Organization 'to take the necessary steps... for restoring peace in the area ...'. In 1956, the year of Suez, UN Secretary-General Hammarskjöld was asked to organize 'any measures which ... would reduce the existing tensions'. In 1958, Hammarskjöld was asked 'to make ... practical arrangements ... to help in upholding the purposes and principles of the Charter in relation to Lebanon and Jordan'. In 1967, after the June war, Gunnar Jarring was designated Special Representative of the UN Secretary-General 'to promote agreement and assist efforts to achieve a peaceful and accepted settlement'. In 1973, after the October war, the Security Council decided that negotiations should begin immediately 'under appropriate auspices aimed at establishing a just and durable peace'.

In 1991, negotiations for a settlement of the Palestine question were initiated outside the UN framework at a conference in Madrid under the formal sponsorship of the United States and the Russian Federation. In 1993 a partial agreement was reached between Israel and the Palestine Liberation Organization through the good offices of Norway.

The above-mentioned UN decisions about the Palestine question were all applications of the Articles of the Charter on the peaceful settlement of disputes, but a variety of organs were used, and considerable discretion was allowed about the precise form which third-party assistance would take.

If UN policymaking organs are unable to reach agreement, it is tempting to transfer the problem to the Secretary-General. Dag Hammarskjöld, Secretary-General from 1953 to 1961, was often entrusted with broad responsibilities and considerable discretion. He was a great innovator. He seemed to relish the chance to have goals in general terms set by policymaking organs, but leaving him considerable latitude about how the goals were to be pursued and such matters as the order in which different aspects would be taken up and the extent to which issues would be separated or joined.

Hammarskjöld took the view, as did his predecessor and successors, that the UN Secretary-General enjoys considerable diplomatic and operational discretion, arising from his responsibilities under Article 99 of the Charter. The Secretary-General is entrusted by the Charter with many straightforward administrative duties (see, for example, Arts. 12(2), 20, 97, and 98). Article 99, on the other hand, confers on him a non-administrative responsibility: that of drawing the Security Council's attention to 'any matter which in his opinion may threaten the maintenance of international peace and security'. To do this, a Secretary-General needs to keep his finger on the pulse of world politics, to appoint staff, make visits, receive reports, and undertake many functions which are implied in the concept of the Office of Secretary-General – not his material office on the 38th floor of the UN Headquarters building in Manhattan, but the rights and responsibilities inhering in the Office of Secretary-General.

When policymaking organs failed to agree, it was tempting to 'leave it to Dag'. Since the Hammarskjöld era, the policymaking organs have not hesitated to entrust vital tasks to successive Secretaries-General, but often without giving them the resources in money and personnel or diplomatic backing that they were entitled to expect. Moreover, the Secretaries-General have taken a broad view of their responsibilities and have not hesitated to undertake independent initiatives within the framework of the Charter.

The ability of the Secretaries-General to fulfil their duties under Article 99 of the Charter relies on effective collection and analysis of information by the UN Secretariat. This is currently undertaken by regional desks within the Department for Political Affairs.

Trygve Lie of Norway, the first Secretary-General, described his post as 'the most impossible job on this earth'. He was not exaggerating. Successive Secretaries-General have all stressed the importance of the implied duties under Article 99, and Secretary-General Waldheim exercised his power under Article 99 to convene the Security Council in order to deal with the problem of US diplomatic hostages in Tehran.

It should be noted that the powers of the General Assembly and the Security Council regarding disputes or situations are limited to the making of recommendations (Arts. 14, 33(2), 36(1), and 37). Neither organ has the power to impose a settlement, unless the dispute or situation escalates so as to become a threat to or breach of the peace, or an act of aggression takes place, in which event Chapter VII of the Charter comes into force and the Security Council may decide on preventive or enforcement measures. The General Assembly may draw the Security Council's attention to 'situations which are likely to endanger international peace and security' (Arts. 10(2) and 11(3)), thus paralleling the Secretary-General's express powers under Article 99.

If all efforts at peaceful settlement fail and the problem escalates, the Security Council has at its disposal a graduated series of coercive measures. The least coercive action is under Article 40, in order to prevent an aggravation of the situation, and is called 'provisional measures'. These are 'without prejudice to the rights, claims, or position' of the parties concerned. Provisional measures have in practice included such acts as to call for the cessation of military action, the withdrawal of military units, the demarcation of lines of separation of forces, the establishment of demilitarized zones, the release of prisoners, embargoes on the introduction of new military supplies or personnel, and procedures for the prevention of infiltration and armed incidents. Two peace observation missions, those in Kashmir and the Middle East, have sometimes been regarded as within the scope of Article 40, but it is perhaps bordering on the absurd to regard measures which have been in force for 48 years as 'provisional'. (The Security Council's rules of procedure are still provisional!)

Article 40 on provisional measures is preceded by an Article which enables the Security Council to make a formal determination that there has been a threat to or breach of the peace or an act of aggression; and if such a formal determination is made, the tendency has been to regard the concurrent or subsequent decisions as binding on the parties.

If provisional measures fail, the Security Council may move to the next stage of coercion, which comprises non-military measures of enforcement (Art. 41). These are measures to give effect to the Council's earlier decisions and may comprise partial or total economic sanctions, interruption of communications, and severance of diplomatic relations.

Since 1990 the Security Council has increasingly utilized the tool of imposing partial sanctions on a state to force compliance. These have been imposed on Libya to seek the handing-over of Libyan nationals alleged to have bombed American and French aircraft; against Iraq to force compliance with UN weapons inspections; and against the UNITA faction in Angola. This was a rare example of sanctions against a sub-state actor following UNITA's refusal to accept the UN-verified election result. An oil embargo was imposed against Haiti, and varying degrees of sanctions were imposed against Serbia, Montenegro, and the other Republics of former Yugoslavia.

The third stage envisaged in the Charter, to be taken if non-military measures would be or have been inadequate, comprises military action, including demonstrations and blockade, provided for under Article 42 of the Charter. Military action was authorized for Korea in 1950, in the Congo 'if necessary' in 1961, by the United Kingdom to prevent oil from reaching Southern Rhodesia in 1966 (the Beira patrol), to enforce the Council's resolutions that Iraq should withdraw from Kuwait in 1990, to facilitate the delivery of relief supplies in Somalia in 1992–94, and in Bosnia in 1993–94. It will be seen that the first four Articles of Chapter VII have operated much as the founders envisaged, and the same is true of the last

Article of the Chapter concerning 'the inherent right of individual or collective self-defence'. Articles 43 to 48, on the other hand, have been largely inoperative because, as noted in Chapters 1 and 3, the great powers were unable to agree on the kinds and control of forces to be placed at the disposal of the Security Council; and Members have not been regularly informed about action under Article 51.

Peace-keeping is not expressly provided for in the Charter. The crux of traditional peace-keeping has been to use a symbol of world authority and concern, not as a means of military coercion, but for tranquillizing a troubled frontier or demilitarized zone or for keeping law and order in a disturbed region. An essential condition of UN peace-keeping is the consent of the host country. Sir Brian Urquhart, who served in the UN Secretariat for more than 40 years, has written that

> Peace-keeping depends on the non-use of force and on political symbolism. It is the projection of the principle of non-violence on to the military plane. It requires discipline, initiative, objectivity, and leadership, as well as ceaseless supervision and political direction.

The first UN Emergency Force was not designed or refined in a research institute or in the research section of a government department, as was, for instance, nuclear deterrence. Anthony Eden had said in the House of Commons during the Suez crisis that British forces were in the Canal zone to separate the belligerents and prevent a renewal of hostilities. If the United Nations were willing to take over these tasks, he said, nobody would be more pleased than the British. Lester Pearson of Canada seized the opportunity and immediately thought up the idea of a UN Force to replace the military forces of the intervening states. Hammarskjöld viewed this idea with some apprehension, but he eventually came to understand that the proposal was worth pursuing. Until this point, he had been obsessed with other ideas: finding fault with Israel, opening the Suez Canal which had become

TABLE 4.1   UN peace-keeping operations

Title	Abbreviation	Area	Date Established	Date Terminated
UN Truce Supervision Organization	UNTSO	Middle East	1948	Present
UN Military Observer Group in India and Pakistan	UNMOGIP	Jammu and Kashmir	1949	Present
UN Emergency Force	UNEF	Sinai	1956	1967
UN Observer Group in Lebanon	UNOGIL	Lebanon	1958	1958
UN Operation in the Congo	ONUC	Congo	1960	1964
UN Observers and Security Force in West Irian	UNSF	West Irian	1962	1963
UN Yemen Observation Mission	UNYOM	Yemen	1963	1964
UN Peacekeeping Force in Cyprus	UNFICYP	Cyprus	1964	Present
UN India-Pakistan Observer Mission	UNIPOM	India and Pakistan	1965	1966
Representative of the Secretary-General in the Dominican Republic	DOMREP	Dominican Republic	1965	1966
Second UN Emergency Force in the Middle East	UNEF II	Sinai	1973	1979
UN Disengagement Force	UNDOF	Golan Heights	1974	Present
UN Interim Force in Lebanon	UNIFIL	Southern Lebanon	1978	Present
UN Good Offices Mission in Afghanistan	UNGOMAP	Afghanistan	1988	1990

Title	Abbreviation	Area	Date Established	Date Terminated
UN Iran–Iraq Military Observer Group	UNIIMOG	Iran–Iraq	1988	1992
UN Transition Assistance Group in Namibia	UNTAG	Namibia	1989	1990
UN Observer Group in Central America	ONUCA	Central America	1989	1992
UN Observer Group for the Verification of the Elections in Haiti	ONUVEH	Haiti	1990	1991
UN Angola Verification Mission	UNAVEM	Angola	1989	1991
UN Angola Verification Mission	UNAVEM II	Angola	1991	Present
UN Mission for the Referendum in Western Sahara	MINURSO	Western Sahara	1991	Present
UN Observer Mission in El Salvador	ONUSAL	El Salvador	1991	Present
UN Iraq–Kuwait Observer Mission	UNIKOM	Iraq–Kuwait border	1991	Present
UN Advance Mission in Cambodia	UNAMIC	Cambodia	1991	1992
UN Transitional Authority in Cambodia	UNTAC	Cambodia	1992	1993
UN Observer Mission in South Africa	UNOMSA	South Africa	1992	Present
UN Operation in Mozambique	ONUMOZ	Mozambique	1992	Present
UN Operation in Somalia	UNOSOM	Somalia	1992	1993

continued on page 64

TABLE 4.1   continued

Title	Abbreviation	Area	Date Established	Date Terminated
UN Protection Force	UNPROFOR	Croatia, Bosnia and the Former Yugoslav Republic of Macedonia	1992	Present
UN Operation in Somalia	UNOSOM II	Somalia	1993	Present
UN Observer Mission in Georgia	UNOMIG	Georgia	1993	Present
UN Observer Mission in Liberia	UNOMIL	Liberia	1993	Present
UN Observer Mission in Uganda–Rwanda	UNOMUR	Border between Uganda and Rwanda	1993	1993
UN Mission in Haiti	UNMIH	Haiti	1993	Present
UN Assistance Mission for Rwanda	UNAMIR	Rwanda	1993	Present

blocked during the fighting, the care of Palestine refugees, and so on. These were all worthwhile or necessary objectives, but none were designed to persuade the invaders to withdraw. Over a lunch meeting, Pearson wore away Hammarskjöld's scepticism. When the first vote came in the General Assembly, Pearson cast a tactical abstention and then produced his own plan for a UN Force to replace the invaders. This was approved by an overwhelmingly favourable vote. In this unplanned way some great ideas are born. Hammarskjöld was won over and became one of the keenest advocates of the first UN Force.

This first UN Emergency Force (UNEF I) served several purposes. It symbolized the concern of the international community; its presence at the scene of the trouble had a tranquillizing effect on the parties; the invaders were enabled to withdraw from an untenable situation; the opposing forces were prevented from assaulting each other without first assaulting the United Nations. The peak complement of UNEF was 6000 officers and men. It was not sent to the Middle East to fight anyone or to change the military or political situation, and it was instructed to use force only in self-defence.

There were certain similarities between the Suez and Hungarian crises in 1956. Both questions arose first in the Security Council; in both cases action by the Security Council was prevented by the use of the veto; both questions were thereupon transferred to the General Assembly under an emergency procedure; in both cases the Assembly called for a cessation of hostilities and the withdrawal of foreign troops.

But there the similarity ends. The Soviet attitude regarding Hungary never wavered. The Soviet Government was not disposed to modify its policy on a question it regarded as vital to its security. Neither the UN Secretary-General nor an observer group nominated by him, nor a committee of inquiry established by the General Assembly, were permitted to visit Hungary. The Security Council, the General Assembly, and the Secretary-General adhered throughout to certain positions of principle, but this had no discernible effect on the outcome.

In the Suez case, two processes were at work. Diplomatic pressure was exerted, both through the United Nations and by other means, for the withdrawal of foreign forces from Egypt. At the same time, the United Nations entered upon a major police action in which an international UN Force replaced the invading armies with the consent of the nations concerned. When Egyptian consent was withdrawn in 1967, the UN Force departed.

It is difficult to plan precisely the composition or operation of United Nations forces. Important precedents were created when UNEF was set up in 1956, but when another crisis arose in the Middle East two years later, a quite different form of UN presence was needed. Lebanon had complained to the United Nations of interference in its internal affairs by the United Arab Republic (Egypt), and the Security Council decided to set up an observation group to prevent illegal infiltration across the Lebanese borders. The observation group in Lebanon was not a 'Force', even of a police type. At its maximum it consisted of some 600 observers, mainly military officers, drawn from 21 countries, and equipped with reconnaissance vehicles and aircraft.

UNEF I should be distinguished both from the Unified Command in Korea and the UN-authorised coalition to liberate Kuwait, on the one hand, and UN observation missions such as those in Kashmir, the Middle East, Lebanon, Yemen, and India–Pakistan. Peace-keeping contingents are seconded national contingents for interposition between the belligerents in order to deter violations of the ceasefire, whereas the members of observer missions were individually recruited, were stationed at fixed posts, and simply recorded violations. UNEF was a remarkable invention, and most of the principles on which it was based have stood the test of time.

In the light of Hammarskjöld's experience in establishing UN peace-keeping in the Middle East in 1956, and U Thant's experience in Cyprus in 1964, a number of principles were evolved governing UN peace-keeping operations.

(1) The purpose of UN peace-keeping is to prevent an outbreak or recurrence of fighting and to assist in maintaining law and order.

(2) The United Nations cannot station military peace-keeping units on the territory of a state without the consent of the government concerned.

(3) The UN Secretary-General is responsible for appointing a Peace-keeping Force commander and for establishing and directing the Force, in accordance with the decisions of the policy-making organ concerned.

(4) It is for the United Nations alone to decide on the size and composition of any Peace-keeping Force,

taking fully into account the views of the host country and other states directly concerned. (Communist bloc countries were originally opposed in principle to UN peace-keeping, but in 1973 Poland provided a contingent for the UN operation in Sinai, and on the Golan Heights in 1974.)

(5) In the case of UNEF, Hammarskjöld took the position that the UN Force should not include units from any of the five permanent members of the Security Council or from any country which might be considered as having a special interest in the situation. This principle was modified in 1960 when several African contingents having an interest in the Congo (Zaire) were included in the UN operation, in 1964 when British contingents in Cyprus were brought within the UN operation, and in 1982 when French forces served in the UN Force in Lebanon.

(6) In the light of some unfortunate episodes in the Congo, U Thant maintained for Cyprus that the national contingents comprising the Peace-keeping Force were integral parts of it and took their orders only from the Force commander: the personnel of UN Peace-keeping Forces are under the exclusive command and control of the United Nations at all times.

(7) The personnel of a UN Peace-keeping Force should be loyal to the aims of the Organization. UN personnel cannot be a party to any internal conflict, and a UN Peace-keeping Force should not be used to enforce any specific political solution or to influence the political balance, except through the restoration of quiet and the creation of an improved climate in which political solutions may be sought. UN personnel should act with restraint and complete impartiality towards local communities, and should refrain from expressing publicly any opinion on the political problems of the host country.

(8) The operations of a Force are separate from but complementary to UN mediation or other peace-making.

(9) A UN Peace-keeping Force does not engage in combat activities, though it may respond with force if attacked or to maintain the viability of the operation. UN Peace-Keeping Forces should have full freedom of movement and all facilities necessary for their tasks. They may resist by force any attempts to compel them to withdraw from positions they occupy. Should all peaceful means of persuasion fail and the use of armed force be necessary, advance warning should be given where possible, the principle of minimum force should always be applied, and fire should continue only as long as necessary to achieve its immediate aim. (In the Congo, the Security Council authorized the UN Force 'to take vigorous action, including the requisite measure of force, if necessary', for specified and limited purposes.)

(10) In the case of UNEF, Hammarskjöld's initial view was that the costs should be allocated among UN Members according to the normal scale of budgetary contributions. When the Soviet bloc and France objected to this principle, other methods were used in Suez and later operations such as sharing the costs between the parties (West Irian) or voluntary governmental contributions (Cyprus). The ideal way of paying for peacemaking or peace-keeping operations would be by allocating the expenses according to the usual scale of assessments, which is based on ability to pay (Art. 17.2).

During the 1980s and early 1990s, UN peace-keeping grew considerably. More UN operations were launched after 1990 than in the previous forty years. Initially, UN operations grew in complexity, with mandates ranging from the supervision of election verification (e.g. the UN Observer Mission in El Salvador) to mine-clearing and civilian administration (e.g. the UN Transitional Authority in Cambodia), while maintaining the UNFICYP principles of impartiality and consent. In the mid-1990s the Security Council established a number of peace-keeping operations with mandates derived from Chapter VII of the Charter, where perceptions of consent and, in a few cases, impartiality are more blurred. The UN Operations in Bosnia (UNPROFOR) and Somalia (UNOSOM II) were initially intended to allow a ceasefire to become effective, not to monitor an existing ceasefire, and to create a safe environment for the passage of humanitarian aid, but both soon became embroiled in wider problems.

Peacemaking and peace-keeping are necessary, but both have their limitations. The adoption of a resolution by a UN policymaking organ usually seems to governments to mark the end of a phase; for the UN Secretariat it is almost always the beginning of a new phase. In the economic and social field there has developed a useful link between research and analysis, on the one hand, and field operations, on the other, but this has been less true in the political field. Efforts to develop systematic techniques for dealing with political crises have been proposed from time to time, but with only limited success. The United Nations nearly always rises to the occasion if there is a real crisis, but it often gives the impression of improvising.

The 'peace' which the United Nations seeks to maintain is precarious. Indeed, it is one of the paradoxes of the UN system that one way of getting international attention is to endanger world peace. While it is no doubt an exaggeration to assert, as did one UN delegate, that the United Nations Charter is 'a standing invitation to violence', the fact remains that discontent sometimes becomes a matter of international concern only when it erupts into violence.

5 Disarmament

The word 'disarmament' has a high emotional content. To some people it signifies the state of military unpreparedness which characterized the European democracies during the time when Nazi Germany was growing in strength, an attitude of appeasement and moral surrender, an attempt to substitute pious slogans for the realities of power. At the other extreme are those who think of disarmament as a simple cure for all international ills, a cure which is beyond the reach of human beings only because of the selfishness or stupidity of a few soldiers, scientists, arms-dealers, or diplomats.

The kind of disarmament which has been considered by UN organs, and with which we are concerned in this chapter, would not require that any nation or group of nations should be placed in a position of weakness while other nations remain strong. International disarmament would no doubt involve risks, but so does international armament: there is no policy without risk.

But equally it should be emphasized that the case for disarmament is damaged if too many things, or the wrong things, are claimed for it. To reduce, destroy, or redeploy weapons does not necessarily lead to a diminution of international tension. Unilateral disarmament by one nation or by a group of nations might have important moral or political consequences, but if it is not carried out in a way that maximizes the likelihood of reciprocity, it may simply add to insecurity. An international agreement or unilateral decision to disarm is no panacea: it is a course of action designed to diminish specific dangers. The main purposes of international disarmament are to reduce the particular risks of war which arise from the existence and nature of weapons and not, directly, the risks arising from the political and other conditions which lead nations to make military preparations; to save money; to

71

avoid unnecessary suffering and destruction if war should occur; and to facilitate war-termination.

During the past four decades, there has been a tendency in the West to prefer the concept of arms control rather than disarmament. Arms control has a simpler purpose than disarmament: it is to maintain or increase military stability. When nations negotiate about weapons, it is not necessary that they should declare in advance whether their aim is disarmament or arms control. Indeed, they may not have decided at the outset which goal will provide greater security.

Disarmament, then, is a process or action, following a negotiated agreement or undertaken and declared unilaterally, whereby weapons already in existence are dismantled or destroyed or the materials are diverted to peaceful uses. Arms control is a process or action to prohibit or limit the testing, manufacture, stockpiling, transfer, deployment or use of specified weapons, or to use them only in reprisal or other defined circumstances.

One of the difficulties encountered in negotiation about weapons arises from the fact that nations of similar size may, for reasons of geography and history, deploy different kinds of military force. An island like Mauritius is likely to have a navy, while a landlocked country like Zimbabwe will give priority to land and air forces. Even when countries have defence forces of similar characteristics and scale, there will be tangible asymmetries to take into account. Are military formations of identical size? A German armoured division has twice as many men and tanks as its British equivalent. A US airborne division has more than twice as many men as the Russian equivalent. And how is it possible to establish equivalences between different weapons and military capabilities? How many high-yield but relatively inaccurate nuclear bombs dropped by gravity from aircraft are equal to how many lower-yield but relatively accurate nuclear missiles launched from fixed silos? How can one compare a missile with one warhead, a missile with several warheads which can be directed at only a single target, and a missile with several warheads which can be directed independently at different targets? How is it possible to take account of less tangible factors like secrecy, discipline, reliability of equipment, and speed of maintenance?

Negotiation about arms would make greater progress if it were possible to distinguish between offensive forms of military power (first-strike weapons), which could be progressively reduced and then totally eliminated, and retaliatory and defensive weapons. Unfortunately, military technologists have developed versatile weapons-systems. Whether a long-range missile with a nuclear warhead is first-strike or second-strike would depend on the circumstances in which it was used. Moreover, the Western concept of deterrence included the conditional intention to use weapons of mass destruction first in the event of extreme provocation or an actual attack with conventional weapons. The nuclear deterrent was not a means of resisting aggression: it was an attempt to prevent aggression from taking place by threatening to retaliate if it did, by whatever means and on whatever scale is necessary. Deterrence does not always work. The fact that four members of the Coalition defending Kuwait had nuclear weapons (Britain, France, the United States and the Russian Federation) did not deter the original aggression, nor induce Iraq to withdraw without a war with conventional weapons, shows that nuclear weapons are of limited utility, especially if the other side has usable biological or chemical weapons.

The threat of nuclear retaliation will not deter if it is not credible. This does not mean that the exercise of retaliation in case of provocation or attack must be absolutely certain, only that there must be enough risk of its being exercised to make it unwise to provoke it. The actual use of the nuclear deterrent would obviously be an admission that deterrence had failed, and it would doubtless provoke counter-retaliation. The doctrine of nuclear deterrence theoretically requires that, as a last resort, nuclear war would be preferable in certain circumstances to any conceivable alternative.

The doctrine of deterrence, indeed all military planning, must presuppose that leaders of other nations are more likely to behave rationally than irrationally. There are, however, dangers of war in addition to a deliberate attack by an adversary, which is why nations take precautions against war by accident, misunderstanding or miscalculation. This risk has, of course, always existed. Indeed, there is a sense in which just about every war in modern times arose from one or other of these circumstances. In pre-nuclear times, however, it was at least theoretically possible to go into reverse in the event of war by mistake, or to win such a war, or to lose but live to fight another day. But modern weapons are delivered so fast and with such deadly accuracy, and are so destructive in their effects, that it is no longer reasonable to rely on responses which were reasonable in pre-nuclear days. There is a point beyond which nuclear weapons, once the decision to launch them has been taken, cannot be recalled; and there would be no victor in any intelligible sense in an all-out nuclear war. Moreover, every war between nuclear powers would be potentially a nuclear war, and the risks increase as nuclear weapons are more widely disseminated.

The nuclear powers have, no doubt, taken elaborate precautions to prevent the accidental detonation of nuclear devices. It is also possible to take steps to reduce, though not to eliminate completely, the danger of war by misunderstanding by such devices as hot-lines linking capitals. But it is impossible to eliminate entirely the risk of war by miscalculation, since this possibility is an inevitable part of the human condition.

In addition to nuclear weapons, there are two other groups of weapons of mass destruction: chemical weapons (CW, poisons) and bacteriological/biological weapons (BW, germs). The treaty on BW (Table 5.1, no. 7) did not provide for verification. The more recent treaty on CW (Table 5.1, no. 25) included provisions for destruction of stocks and limited provisions for verification.

The never-ending competition in the development of

TABLE 5.1   Some major arms control and disarmament
agreements

	No. of parties (signatories only in nos 12, 13, 14, 17, and 24)
1. Antarctic Treaty, 1959	40
2. Partial test ban treaty, prohibiting nuclear tests in the atmosphere, outer space, and underwater, 1963	120
3. Outer space treaty, 1967	93
4. Treaty of Tlatelolco prohibiting nuclear weapons in Latin America, 1967	24
5. Nuclear Non-proliferation Treaty, 1968	156
6. Treaty prohibiting the emplacement of weapons on the sea-bed and ocean floor, 1971	88
7. Convention prohibiting bacteriological (biological) weapons and toxins, 1972	126
8. Interim Agreement, Protocol, and agreed interpretations on the limitation of strategic offensive arms (SALT I), 1972	2
9. Anti-Ballistic Missiles Treaty, 1972	2
10. Establishment of Standing Consultative Commission, 1972	2
11. Protocol to the ABM Treaty, 1974	2
12. Threshold treaty and Protocol on underground nuclear tests, 1974	2
13. Declaration of Ayachuco, 1974	9
14. Treaty and Protocol on peaceful nuclear explosions, 1976	2
15. Convention prohibiting environmental modification for military purposes, 1977	59
16. Guidelines for nuclear transfers (the London Club), 1977	28
17. Treaty, Protocol, agreed statements, common understandings, and agreed memorandum on the limitation of strategic offensive arms (SALT II), 1979	2
18. Agreement on the moon and other celestial bodies, 1979	7
19. Convention prohibiting the use of inhumane or indiscriminate weapons, 1981	35
20. Treaty of Rarotonga (South Pacific), 1985	11

continued on page 76

TABLE 5.1 continued

	No. of parties (signatories only in nos 12, 13, 14, 17, and 24)
21. Intermediate-range Nuclear Forces Treaty, 1988	2
22. Strategic Arms Reduction Treaty (START I), 1991	5
23. Conventional Forces in Europe, 1992	29
24. Chemical Weapons Convention, 1993	*
25. Strategic Arms Reduction Treaty (START II), 1993	*

* These treaties had not entered into force at the time of going to press.

Source: Adapted from Bailey, S. D., *War and Conscience in the Nuclear Age* (Macmillan, 1987), p. 144, and the SIPRI *Yearbook 1993*, pp. 549–54, 576–89, 710 and 763.

weapons means that an arms race may acquire a momentum of its own. The technical experts feel impelled to transform each new theoretical possibility into an actuality, and military planners decide afterwards what its use or justification should be. Each side, on the basis of intelligence which may be incomplete or faulty, over-reacts to the supposed developments on the other side.

In arms negotiations, it is useful to distinguish between conventional weapons, chemical weapons (poisons), biological weapons (germs), and nuclear weapons; and nuclear weapons may be subdivided by range, yield or method of delivery. The Geneva Protocol, which bans the use in war of poisons and germs, has been in existence for 70 years, but the Western powers have always resisted proposals to ban the use of nuclear weapons, believing that the possibility that nuclear weapons will be used is necessary for maintaining deterrence. It should be noted, however, that the UN General Assembly declared in 1961 that the use of nuclear weapons would be inconsistent with the spirit, letter and aims of the United Nations, and also contrary to international law and the laws of humanity. The UN Human Rights Commission expressed a similar opinion in 1984.

It can, of course, be argued that military hardware is neutral: moral and political issues arise only when someone intends, threatens, or decides to use it. At the same time, nuclear and chemical weapons have been used in war, and modern weapons are of such a character that one can understand why the possibility of their use should give rise to feelings of revulsion, and why it seems reasonable to make efforts to prohibit or limit their production, deployment and use. Moreover, *nuclear* weapons seem to be unique in that to test them above ground, even in time of peace, releases radiation which causes tumours, harm to foetuses in the womb, and damage to reproductive organs, leading to physical and/or mental genetic defects in future generations.

If a country wishes to manufacture nuclear weapons, it needs to make or obtain either highly-enriched uranium or plutonium extracted from the spent fuel of a nuclear reactor; the ability to construct a device which will explode by fission or fusion; and the ability to construct a delivery vehicle for conveying the warhead to the target. Most of the basic information for these processes is now available in the open literature, but it is a flight of fantasy to imagine that a usable nuclear weapon can be constructed in a garage or cow-shed. All the same, it is not implausible to speculate that, if present trends continue, there are likely to be a dozen or more nuclear-weapon states by the end of the century, most of the new nuclear powers being in unstable parts of the world. While the manufacture of chemical and biological weapons is within the capacity of many countries, that of nuclear weapons is, at the time of writing, an overt monopoly of half a dozen countries. India has exploded a peaceful nuclear device, but any device that explodes may be directed to a target and used for military purposes.

National proposals on disarmament are no doubt logical and coherent when first drafted in defence and foreign ministries, but they rarely see the light of day in their initial forms. As consultation with other departments of government takes place, the proposals undergo revision: the specific becomes vague, ambiguities appear, important ideas are lost. The resulting compromise must then be discussed with allied and friendly governments. A collection of national compromises eventually becomes a collective allied compromise, in which there are new imprecisions. This allied compromise then meets a compromise from the other side or sides, and negotiations take place, looking towards an international compromise.

There are now a great number of international forums for debate and negotiation about weapons. The UN General Assembly deals with more than 20 items on disarmament and related matters each year, and adopts about 70 resolutions. The UN Disarmament Commission, which, like the General Assembly, consists of all UN Members, is mainly a debating forum. Other UN bodies include *ad hoc* committees on the Indian Ocean, the Committee on the Peaceful Uses of Outer Space, the Scientific Committee on the Effects of Atomic Radiation and the proposed World Disarmament Conference. The negotiating body in Geneva, known as the Conference on Disarmament, reports to the UN General Assembly and is serviced by UN staff, but it is, strictly speaking, not a UN body. The conferences under the auspices of the Helsinki accords are mainly for debate on general principles governing security, confidence-building, and disarmament in Europe.

Weapons are a symptom of mistrust. Once the mistrust is removed, the weapons become unnecessary. There are no defence forces on either side of the land frontier between Holland and Belgium, or in the sea and air between Australia and New Zealand. But negotiations for international agreements on weapons proceed on the assumption that arms should be regulated or reduced or even eliminated while mistrust continues – indeed, precisely because there is mistrust. Disarmament in this context thus requires some method or combination of methods for giving confidence that international obligations to disarm are being honoured. In a world of fallible human beings and machines, such methods of verification can never provide a completely foolproof guarantee that violations will never occur. All they can do is to make cheating as risky as possible. Even with the best detection system or systems, there will always remain a theoretical possibility that one party to an agreement on disarmament could cheat to a small extent, and get away with it; witness Iraq and North Korea. Governments often believe that other governments have taken unfair advantage of ambiguous provisions in agreements. So governments, if they are realistic, not only ask whether cheating is theoretically possible but also whether, in any particular set of circumstances, the risks of cheating are greater or less than the risks of entering or not entering into a disarmament agreement.

Arms are not only a symptom of mistrust, they may also be a cause of it – witness the Cuban missile crisis and the difficulties over the neutron bomb and intermediate-range missiles in Europe. Arms races are always expensive and usually destabilizing. Negotiation is needed, not only in the hope of concluding agreements, but because the very process of negotiating about arms control and disarmament provides a means of communication between potential adversaries about those policies and actions which give rise to anxiety and so lead to overreaction. The exchange of information during negotiations helps each party to adjust those defence postures which the other side finds provocative, and to do so without impairing its own security.

For the first four decades of the nuclear era the Soviet Union gave the impression that it accepted with great reluctance the necessity for effective inspection. Secrecy is an important military asset, and because of the nature of Soviet society, it was a more valuable asset to the Soviet Union than it was to the West. If the Soviet bloc was to retain this military advantage it had to press for a form of inspection which did not permit other states to use international inspection for disarmament as a means of acquiring significant information about those military dispositions not covered by the agreement. At the same time, there was an inescapable logic in the Western view that the only way to be reasonably certain that both sides were honouring their obligations was to check 'remainders' rather than 'destructions'.

Three types of verification can be used:

(1) international, such as the safeguards procedures of the International Atomic Energy Agency or UN inspection of the zones of limited armaments on the Golan Heights between Israel and Syria;

(2) regional, as under the 1954 Protocol to the Brussels Treaty, whereby the German Federal Republic undertook not to manufacture atomic, biological or chemical weapons on its territory, or the Treaty of Tlatelolco on the denuclearization of Latin America;

(3) bilateral, as under various agreements between the superpowers on nuclear weapons.

Traditionally, it was assumed that inspection should be 'on-site', as is provided for in some treaties. In the past 25 years, however, science and technology have provided new methods of verification by photo-reconnaissance, radar, seismic detectors, and other long-distance technologies, now usually known as 'national technical means'. Most disarmament or arms control agreements provide for consultative procedures among the parties to promote the objectives of the treaty or to deal with ambiguous activities or alleged breaches.

The nature of the nuclear dilemma has driven people to hope that war can be limited, and there are several varieties of the theory of limited war. One school of thought would regard wars fought for certain purposes (such as wars of national liberation) as permissible and other kinds as impermissible. Others would favour prohibiting the use of the more destructive or cruel weapons (chemical, biological, nuclear or radiological), considering their use as too barbarous for use by civilized belligerents,

however righteous the cause. Others, again, would ban
the use of weapons for certain purposes, such as to ter-
rorize non-combatants. The doctrine of the just war, which
is held by many non-pacifist Christians, seeks to establish limits on the purposes for which wars are fought
and the means used to achieve military victory. While it
is prudent and humane to seek agreements on limiting
war-fighting capabilities, we can never be sure that limited wars will not escalate. Indeed, it has been said that
if ever nations were to become sufficiently rational to agree
to limit war, they would probably find that they could
agree to abolish it.

Periods of progress and immobility over disarmament
have alternated since the Second World War. The Soviet
Union, as it then was, initially advocated the complete
banning of nuclear weapons and proportionate cuts in
other arms, while the United States advocated international
ownership and control of nuclear facilities, and took the
line that disarmament of conventional weapons could not
begin until states had verified the declarations by the
other side of precisely how many military personnel and
weapons they disposed of. Serious negotiations took place
in 1954–55, following the Soviet acceptance, as a basis
for negotiation, of an Anglo-French proposal providing
for an immediate ban on the use of nuclear weapons except
in defence against aggression, and a phased programme
of disarmament, linking conventional and nuclear weapons,
with appropriate measures of control. In 1955 the Soviet
Union submitted a detailed, comprehensive, and far-reaching counter-proposal, including a greater degree of verification than had previously been acceptable to Soviet
leaders but less than was then thought necessary by the
West.

The next phase was relatively unproductive, except for
the conclusion in 1961 of an agreement between the two
superpowers on the principles to govern disarmament,
negotiated by John McCloy and Valerian Zorin. Many of
these principles are still valid after the lapse of more
than 30 years, though the set as a whole now seems too

simplistic, logical and coherent for dealing with such a complex problem, and there are some notable gaps (chemical and biological weapons, for example, outer space, the arms trade). The UN statement of the superpowers was approved unanimously by the UN General Assembly.

(1) The purpose should be to put an end to war as an instrument for settling international problems.

(2) Efforts should continue without interruption towards the ultimate goal of 'general and complete disarmament', so that states would have at their disposal only such non-nuclear weapons and forces as may be necessary 'to maintain internal order and protect the personal security of citizens', and for providing agreed manpower for a UN peace force.

(3) Agreed measures of partial disarmament should be undertaken without prejudice to the total programme.

(4) Measures of disarmament should be balanced so that at no stage should a state or group of states gain military advantage, and so that equal security would be ensured for all.

(5) Disarmament should proceed by stages and within agreed time limits.

(6) Disarmament should be under 'strict and effective international control ... within the framework of the United Nations', with unrestricted and veto-free access to all places as necessary to verify with firm assurance that parties are honouring their obligations.

(7) Progress in disarmament should be accompanied by measures to strengthen the institutions for the peaceful settlement of international disputes and by effective arrangements to deter or suppress any threat or use of armed force in violation of UN purposes and principles. States should place agreed manpower for an international peace force at the disposal of the United Nations.

The United States attached an addendum to point 6, to the effect that verification should be of weapons and forces limited or reduced, and also of forces and weapons retained at each stage. The Soviet Union, while advocating 'effective control over disarmament', was resolutely opposed to 'control over armaments'. In other words, the Soviet Union advocated verification of weapons given up, the United States of weapons left.

The period of relative stalemate which began in 1955 came to an end in 1963 with the conclusion of the partial ban on nuclear tests (Table 5.1, no. 2), for which Harold Macmillan deserved much credit. This was followed by 14 other agreements in the 1960s and 1970s culminating in the SALT II agreement of 1979 (Table 5.1, no. 17). This was strongly opposed by the Reagan Administration, and the US Senate never agreed to its ratification.

When the NATO countries agreed to the deployment in Europe of cruise and Pershing II missiles, partly in response to the deployment of Soviet SS-20 missiles and partly to strengthen the coupling between US and European security, stress was laid on the need to reduce intermediate-range nuclear weapons by the two sides. For several years the United States and the Soviet Union made proposals on the control of weapons, some quite far-reaching. For a time the Soviet Union suspended the testing of nuclear weapons and invited the United States to take reciprocal action, but without success. In 1983 President Reagan issued his plan for space-based defence against missiles, an interesting example of a defensive measure adding to rather than reducing international tension for a time. By the end of 1986 relations between the two superpowers were beginning to improve, and a new and productive disarmament period began to take shape in 1987.

Apart from the arms control or disarmament resulting from international agreements, it is possible for nations to take unilateral steps, either for moral reasons or to increase military stability or in the hope that others will reciprocate. Charles Osgood proposed a set of eight principles designed to maximize the chances of reciprocation of unilateral initiatives.

(1) Each unilateral step must be perceived by the opponent as reducing the external threat. (It is no good simply phasing out naval vessels that are too expensive to run or missiles that have become obsolete.)
(2) Each unilateral step should be accompanied by an explicit invitation to reciprocate.
(3) Unilateral acts should be undertaken whether or not an adversary makes a prior commitment to reciprocate.
(4) Unilateral acts should be planned in sequence and persisted in over substantial periods of time, whether or not an opponent openly reciprocates.
(5) Each step should be announced before it is taken, and given full publicity.
(6) Whenever possible, initiatives should concentrate on areas of mutual interest and opportunities for cooperation.
(7) Steps should be graduated in risk so as to avoid undue dangers during the early period.
(8) Unilateral initiatives should be accompanied by firmness towards the adversary.

If ever major or complete disarmament became a realistic goal, attention would shift to the other measures for resolving conflict after substantial elements of national military power had been eliminated. Can substantial or total disarmament be reconciled with traditional ideas of national sovereignty? How would international disputes be resolved when nations could no longer threaten or use military force? What would be the role of the United Nations and the International Court of Justice, of alliances and regional organizations, in a disarmed world?

The McCloy–Zorin agreement states that progress in disarmament should be accompanied by measures to strengthen institutions for maintaining peace and the settlement of international disputes by peaceful means. It is widely believed that there would be many new problems in a disarmed world, but also that nations will not give up significant amounts of military power until they are assured that adequate peace-making and peace-keeping institutions are in existence or will be established.

In the meantime the vicious circle remains. Should nations seek agreement on disarmament in order to reduce international tension, or should they seek to reduce international tension in order to facilitate agreement on disarmament? As we do not know the answer to this question, it is only realistic to pursue both goals at once.

6 Human Rights

Contrary to popular belief, human rights are not about abstract texts but about people, what they and their neighbours are legally free to do, and what obligations fall on governments for guaranteeing those freedoms. It is often governments that are the main violators of human rights, but individuals and organizations may also violate human rights – for example, when terrorists threaten or harm the innocent for political purposes. From a moral point of view, human rights are about the behaviour of individuals. From a legal point of view, human rights are about the responsibilities of governments.

The UN Charter refers to 'human rights and fundamental freedoms for all' (Arts. 1.(3) and 55c). For example, it is a basic human right that anyone accused of a serious breach of the law is entitled to a fair hearing before an independent and impartial judicial organ. Does that mean, then, that all those accused of serious offences shall be tried by jury? Not at all: many constitutional democracies with fair systems for the administration of justice do not have jury trials, and there is nothing in international or regional treaties on human rights about the right to trial by jury. That is why the suspension of the jury system in Northern Ireland (because of the possible intimidation of jurors and witnesses) does not violate the UK's international obligations.

Another complaint about international or regional work for the protection of human rights is that aggrieved minorities exploit the language of human rights, while forgetting or deliberately concealing the fact that there are no rights without responsibilities. It is true that the language of human rights is often inflated or used for selfish purposes, so that the mere desires or claims of an individual or a group are presented in high-falutin' language as a matter of human rights. The fact that this happens, however, is no reason for disregarding genuine concern for human rights or for failing to make the proper connection between rights and responsibilities.

We are all minorities in some respects, and minorities are entitled to be protected against what Montesquieu called the tyranny of the majority. The founders of the United Nations were farsighted in understanding that concern for human rights cannot be confined within national borders. A fair trial is not simply a privilege for the fortunate citizen of a parliamentary democracy; it is the birthright of every human being.

Moreover, it is sometimes forgotten that the denial of human rights is a frequent cause of armed conflict. Traditionally wars were fought for the dynastic interests of rulers or for access to raw materials or the control of strategic areas. There have been nearly 200 wars since 1945, mostly in the Third World. If one tabulates these wars by causes, one finds that the most frequent cause was the perception that rights were being denied. Any multiple strategy for the prevention of war in the contemporary world should include international concern for human rights – indeed, 'human rights and fundamental freedoms for all without distinction' (Arts. 1(3) and 55c).

The main task of the UN and its agencies has hitherto been international standard-setting, and it has performed that task well. What still needs attention is to secure more effective implementation of the agreed code, so that it will become more and more difficult for citizens to be tyrannized behind the cloak of national sovereignty. The process of implementation, like the verification of disarmament agreements, will involve some intrusion into areas which were traditionally regarded as of domestic concern.

In the UN system, human rights are regarded as social affairs rather than political, and are dealt with each year by the committee of the General Assembly concerned with social, humanitarian, and cultural questions. That is a matter of organizational convenience, and the authors of this concise political guide firmly believe that we should deal with human rights as part of the UN's political role.

Until about a century ago, human rights were regarded as essentially within the domestic jurisdiction of rulers. This traditional view was gradually eroded during the nineteenth century, with campaigns to abolish slavery and the slave trade and to provide humanitarian care for wounded combatants. When the League of Nations came into existence, several new categories of humanitarianism came to be regarded as of international concern, including the protection of minorities and the inhabitants of mandated territories and, through the International Labour Organization, conditions of work throughout the world.

While the machinery thus established was useful within limited fields, it was totally inadequate when it came to outrages against Jews, Gypsies, homosexuals, and political opponents of the Nazi regime in Germany, and this led the wartime Allies to declare in the Atlantic Charter (1941) their determination that people in all lands should in future be able to live free from fear and want. A few months later, in the United Nations Declaration (1942), the allies affirmed the need 'to defend life, liberty, independence, and religious freedom, and to preserve human rights and justice. . . .'

It was natural, therefore, that the politicians and diplomats who assembled in San Francisco in the closing months of the war should want the United Nations to promote and encourage respect for 'the principle of equal rights and self-determination of peoples' and 'human rights and fundamental freedoms for all. . . ' (Arts. 1(2) and (3) and 55). UN Members pledged themselves 'to take joint and separate action' in achieving these purposes (Art. 56), and the Economic and Social Council (ECOSOC) was given the task of making recommendations in this field (Art. 62(2)). The aim of the Trusteeship System was 'self-government or independence as may be appropriate', and other non-self-governing territories outside the Trusteeship System were to develop free political institutions and self-government (Arts. 73(b) and 76(b)).

It was inevitable that the UN machinery for achieving these aims should be complicated. In one of its earliest decisions, ECOSOC established a Human Rights Commission and also a Commission on the Status of Women. In the related field of decolonization, the General Assembly appointed its quota of members of the Trusteeship Council (Art. 86(1)c) and, for colonial territories outside the trusteeship system, a committee to examine information concerning non-self-governing territories (Art. 73(e)). In 1947 the Human Rights Commission established a subsidiary organ composed of individual experts rather than states, charged with the prevention of discrimination and the protection of minorities.

The Human Rights Commission, under the stimulus of Eleanor Roosevelt, widow of Franklin D. Roosevelt, and responding to pressure mainly from religious non-governmental organizations, decided that its first task should be to draft a declaration on human rights, not a treaty with enforceable provisions but a proclamation setting out a common standard for all peoples and all nations. It was the intention of the drafters that the Declaration should be put to the vote in the General Assembly in such a form that states could vote for it as a set of aspirations to be aimed at rather than obligations to be implemented at once. Even this limited goal raised a host of ideological issues between East and West, and between North and South.

The first draft, for example, borrowing ideas from the American Declaration of Independence, had begun, 'All men are brothers. . . '. Following objections from the Commission on the Status of Women over this sexist language, the draft was amended to read, 'All human beings are created free and equal in dignity and rights', followed by the sentence, 'They are endowed by nature with reason and conscience and should act towards one another in a spirit of brotherhood.'

This revised draft raised a new issue, however, because some delegations wanted to change 'endowed by nature' in the second sentence to 'endowed by God', or to add a new sentence to the effect that human beings are created in the image of God. After much debate, those who wanted to mention the Deity withdrew their proposals on the understanding that the second sentence should not ascribe reason and conscience to 'nature'. The text finally agreed simply affirms that human beings are endowed with reason and conscience, without identifying the source of these attributes.

Another issue now arose, because South Africa could not then agree that all human beings are born free and equal, or that everyone should be entitled to all the rights and freedoms set forth in the Declaration. South Africa considered that a person's dignity would not be impaired if they were told that they could not reside in a particular area. South Africa wanted to change 'dignity and rights' to 'fundamental rights and freedoms', but a South African amendment to this effect was defeated. South Africa was also opposed to a sentence in Article 7 providing for 'equal protection against any discrimination', but a South African amendment to delete the sentence was withdrawn when it became clear that virtually all delegations wanted to retain the sentence.

There was much debate about whether the Declaration should be confined to civil and political rights or, as Communist and Third World states would have preferred, should deal comprehensively with economic and social rights as well. In the end, brief provisions were included about social security (Art. 22), the right to work (Art. 23), the right to rest and leisure, 'including . . . periodic holidays with pay' (Art. 24), and the right to an 'adequate standard of living' (Art. 25), and a not wholly satisfactory provision was included to the effect that everyone is entitled to 'a social and international order in which the rights and freedoms set forth in [the] Declaration can be fully realized' (Art. 28).

Saudi Arabia was unhappy about Article 18 on freedom of thought, conscience, and religion, and particularly the assertion of the freedom 'to change . . . religion or belief'. Christian missionaries had often abused the right of residence by becoming forerunners of political intervention, claimed the Saudi delegate, and had been drawn into murderous conflicts because of their efforts to convert local people. Millions of people had been killed in the Crusades and in pointless wars between Catholics and Protestants. The assertion of the right to change one's religion or belief could serve as a pretext for inciting hatred: it was offensive to Muslims. A Saudi proposal to delete the sentence about changing religion or belief was decisively defeated. Saudi Arabia was also worried about Article 16, affirming the right of men and women 'of full age' to marry and found a family, and some of the Catholic countries were uneasy about the assertion of the equal rights of men and women as to marriage, during marriage, 'and at its dissolution'. These provisions were retained, however.

The Communist countries would have liked some mention of the rights of the state. Would the Declaration be used to justify UN intervention in essentially domestic matters? Should not the assertion in Article 17, of the right to own property, take account of the situation in countries where large units of property were publicly owned? Should not the assertion in Article 19 of the right to freedom of opinion and expression be qualified by a condemnation of war-mongering and of the dissemination of fascist ideas? Why did the Declaration contain no reference to the right to decolonization? Proposals to give effect to these ideas were defeated or withdrawn.

Almost as an afterthought, provisions were inserted about duties to the community, limitations on rights for the purpose of assuring the rights and freedoms of others, and non-recognition of any activity aimed at the destruction of rights and freedoms (Arts. 29 and 30).

Eleanor Roosevelt considered the final Declaration good, but not perfect, and this was the general view of the main non-governmental organizations. The Declaration was put to the vote in the General Assembly on 10 December 1948, 48 Members voting in favour and none against, with Saudi Arabia, South Africa, and the Communist

countries abstaining. The tenth of December is now cel-
ebrated each year as Human Rights Day. The Declaration has served as a starting point for subsequent UN
Covenants and Conventions, and it is cited in the consti-
tutions of a number of newly-independent states.

The Declaration was regarded as simply the first stage
in a lengthy process. It established goals, some of them
far-reaching, but nations were free to disregard or postpone the goals, even those countries that had voted in
favour of the Declaration. The next stage was to draft
an enforceable treaty or treaties, elaborating and refin-
ing the Declaration, making the provisions mandatory in
those states that adhered to the new instruments, and
providing for international review of the reports from the
parties and also machinery to deal with petitions from
citizens who believed that their rights had been violated.
The drafting of the new treaty or treaties began in 1949
and was completed in 1966. Three documents emerged
from the drafting process: a Covenant (treaty) on economic, social, and cultural rights; a Covenant on civil and
political rights; and an Optional Protocol (supplementary treaty) providing for individual complaints to a new
Human Rights Committee concerning the denial of civil
and political rights. Under the Covenant on economic,
social and cultural rights, supervision of implementation
was to be by the UN Economic and Social Council, and
this task was at first entrusted to a working group of
states. This procedure proved to be unsatisfactory, and
now the work is handled by a committee composed of
individual experts.

All the issues that had caused controversy over the Declaration of Human Rights in 1946–48 arose again with
the two Covenants, and some new ones as well. One of
the sharpest concerned what became Article 1 of both
Covenants. The admission to UN Membership of a large
number of former colonies meant that there would be
great pressure to affirm the right of self-determination.
The UN Charter describes equal rights and self-determination of peoples as a 'principle' (Arts. 1(2) and 55),

something of value but not an absolute right, because it might in some circumstances conflict with other equally valid principles. In 1960 the General Assembly voted in favour of a declaration, sponsored by the Soviet Union, on the granting of independence to colonial countries and peoples. In that declaration, self-determination of peoples was described as a right, and not simply a principle. Although the 1960 declaration, like most resolutions of the General Assembly, was a recommendation or expression of opinion and therefore not legally binding, it was regarded by Communist and Third World countries as an important advance on the Charter, and it was inconceivable to them that the Covenants on human rights should not build on that advance. The result was that the first Article of the two Covenants affirms that self-determination of peoples is a right, and continues, 'By virtue of that right [peoples] freely determine their political status and freely pursue their economic, social and cultural development.' Much discussion since 1966 has been about what constitutes a people, and whether a people is the same as an ethnic, religious or linguistic minority, whose rights are protected under Article 27 of the Covenant on political rights. The prevailing view is that a homogeneous 'people', forming the majority in a particular area, may exercise self-determination, but that persons belonging to a minority, while not free to exercise self-determination, 'shall not be denied the right, in community with the other members of their group, to enjoy their own culture, to profess and practise their own religion, or to use their own language'. A community may be a people or a minority, but not both.

We turn now from the exceedingly broad subject of human rights to the specific problem of colonialism. Colony is derived from a Latin word meaning 'to cultivate' and in its original form referred to people rather than to the land on which they settled. This use of the word is retained in such expressions as 'a nudist colony' or 'a colony of ants'. In the contemporary political world, however, a colony has usually been thought of as territory

TABLE 6.1   Some major human rights treaties

1. Slavery Convention, amended by Protocol
2. Convention on Freedom of Association and Protection of the Right to Organize
3. Convention on the Prevention and Punishment of the Crime of Genocide
4. Right to Organize and Collective Bargaining Convention
5. Convention for the Suppression of the Traffic in Persons and of the Exploitation of the Prostitution of Others
6. European Convention on Human Rights
7. Equal Remuneration Convention
8. Convention relating to the Status of Refugees
9. Convention on the Political Rights of Women
10. Convention on the International Right of Correction of false or distorted reports in the press
11. Convention relating to the Status of Stateless Persons
12. Supplementary Convention on the Abolition of Slavery, the Slave Trade, and Institutions and Practices similar to Slavery
13. Convention on the Nationality of Married Women
14. Abolition of Forced Labour Convention
15. Discrimination (Employment and Occupation) Convention
16. Convention against Discrimination in Education
17. European Social Charter
18. Convention on the Reduction of Statelessness
19. Convention on Consent to Marriage, Minimum Age for Marriage, and Registration of Marriages
20. Equality of Treatment (Social Security) Convention
21. Social Policy (Basic Aims and Standards) Convention
22. Employment Policy Convention
23. International Convention on the Elimination of all forms of Racial Discrimination
24. International Covenant on Civil and Political Rights
25. International Covenant on Economic, Social, and Cultural Rights
26. Convention on the Non-Applicability of Statutory Limitations to War Crimes and Crimes against Humanity
27. Workers' Representatives Convention
28. Labour Relations (Public Service) Convention
29. Convention on the Elimination of all forms of Discrimination against Women
30. Convention against Torture and other Cruel, Inhuman, or Degrading Treatment or Punishment

in which foreigners have settled and which they administer, directly or indirectly. It is, of course, possible to expand the national boundaries by penetrating and later annexing adjacent areas, but those who engage in this usually think of it as a manifestation of nationalism rather than of colonialism. Indeed, colonialism in the UN has generally meant the process by which Westerners gained and kept control of tropical and semi-tropical areas. The original motive may have been to preach or trade or exploit natural resources or strategic areas: if local conditions became unstable, the foreign settlers were tempted to intervene and eventually to establish their own dominance, sometimes against the wishes of their own metropolitan authorities.

Whatever may have been the initial motive for the acquisition of colonies (and political motives are nearly always mixed), most colonial governments gradually came to manifest some sense of responsibility for the welfare of colonial peoples. What is new in this century is not a sense of international responsibility but the principle of international accountability. The Covenant of the League of Nations and the Charter of the United Nations laid stress on the principle that colonial powers are accountable for the discharge of a sacred trust. But whereas the mandate system of the League of Nations sought to improve the standards of colonial rule, the aim of the United Nations has been to liquidate colonialism entirely.

UN machinery for supervising the administration of colonial territories (and accelerating the ending of colonialism) was from the start separate from general human rights work. The Charter provided for international accountability for two types of dependent territory: those placed under the trusteeship system, with a fair degree of international supervision, and other non-self-governing territories with only a reporting responsibility falling on administering powers.

The effect of UN debate has been to exaggerate the arguments on both sides. That anti-colonialism sometimes takes extreme forms should not obscure the fact that the leaders in any self-respecting nation should wish to run their own affairs. Similarly, the fact that colonialism is sometimes defended in reactionary terms should not obscure legitimate points made by administering powers. It is undoubtedly true, even though some may think it irrelevant, that some of the more outspoken critics of colonialism come from countries in which there is a notable lack of respect for human rights. The Belgian Government, indeed, held that the Charter provisions regarding dependent areas have been interpreted too narrowly. The phrase 'territories whose peoples have not yet attained a full measure of self-government', according to this view, should apply to all non-self-governing peoples, whether they live in colonies or within sovereign states. It was held that the United Nations had been failing in its responsibilities by giving so much attention to Western colonialism and turning a blind eye to other forms of subordinate status.

The elimination of colonialism is usually represented as a struggle between pro-colonial and anti-colonial forces, but colonial powers believed that this was too simple a picture. In their view, the United Nations provided an environment which accelerated a process which was already under way. Indeed, to the extent that Western colonizers spread democratic ideas in dependent areas, they promoted the ending of their superior status.

The fact is that anti-colonialism has been an important and increasingly dominant sentiment since the Second World War, and no Third World state has wished to lay itself open to the charge of being soft on colonialism. As so often happens, the extremists have tended to set the pace. Colonial questions arouse deep passions, and this has obscured the fact that the issue in the United Nations has often been one of pace rather than aim. Colonial powers have contended that it is not in the international interest that power be transferred to indigenous leaders until it is clear that they are ready for political and economic responsibility. Anti-colonialists, on the other hand, have said quite simply that good government is no substitute for self-government. The argument can be pursued endlessly, and in a wider context than that of colonialism.

The role of the United Nations in the elimination of colonialism has, in the main, been an indirect one. The UN's role was direct in the cases of the Congo (Leopold-ville, now Zaire), Indonesia, Israel, West Irian (now part of Indonesia), two former Italian colonies (Libya and Somaliland), and the 11 territories placed under the trusteeship system. In some 80 other cases, however, the role of the UN in the attainment of independence was essentially indirect.

The trusteeship system provided for divided responsibility. *Administration* was to be by an authority, designated in a separate agreement for each trust territory; *supervision* was to be by the United Nations, acting through the General Assembly and the Trusteeship Council (or, in the case of 'strategic' trust territories, the Security Council). The administering authority might in theory be a state or several states or the United Nations itself. In practice, only states have exercised administering responsibilities.

The trusteeship system was voluntary: it did not apply to all colonial territories but only to 'such territories . . . as may be placed thereunder' (Art. 77). The states which placed territories under trusteeship were Australia (in one case, acting on behalf of New Zealand and the UK as well), Belgium, Britain, France, Italy and the USA. South West Africa (known as Namibia since 1969), administered by South Africa, was not brought within the trusteeship system, but all other territories which had been under League of Nations mandate had either become independent or were placed under UN trusteeship. South West Africa had been detached from Germany after the First World War and the mandate awarded to South Africa. In 1946 the South African Government stated that a majority of the territory's inhabitants desired its incorporation with South Africa, but the UN General Assembly would not agree to incorporation.

Namibia was, to all intents and purposes, administered as if it were part of South Africa, and the South African Government maintained that there was no legal obligation to place it under trusteeship. The General Assembly, on the other hand, wished to establish the principle of international accountability for the territory. While there were differences of judgement on legal aspects of the question, the sentiment in UN organs was virtually unanimous in condemning the South African policy of racial discrimination and apartheid.

The International Court of Justice, in response to a request from the General Assembly, advised in 1950 that, while the Charter did not impose a legal obligation on the South African Government to place South West Africa under trusteeship, the territory continued to be under the international mandate assumed by South Africa in 1920 and that the South African Government continued to have international obligations under the League Covenant. In 1971, in another advisory opinion, this time requested by the Security Council, the Court ruled that the continued presence of South Africa in Namibia was illegal, and that UN Members were under an obligation to recognize this illegality and to refrain from helping South Africa to maintain its administration. The Security Council called on the Secretary-General to appoint a Special Representative for Namibia (1978) and the Commander for a UN Transition Assistance Group (UNTAG, 1980). The five Western members of the Security Council constituted themselves as a Contact Group, and they were eventually able to persuade South Africa and SWAPO (South West Africa People's Organisation) to accept a plan which provided for free elections and independence for Namibia. A *de facto* ceasefire took effect in 1988, elections were held under international supervision in 1989, and Namibia attained independence and UN Membership.

An administering authority may designate all or part of a trust territory as a 'strategic area'. This provision was included in the Charter on the initiative of the United States, and only the United States has taken advantage of it. The Pacific islands, detached from Japan after the Second World War, were designated strategic. The trusteeship agreement gave the United States slightly more power regarding matters of security than was granted to the administering authorities of other trust territories, and the United States was allowed to limit the degree of UN supervision in areas closed for reasons of security.

All the territories placed under trusteeship had achieved independence by 1976, except for the Pacific Islands administered by the United States. The Marshall Islands and the Micronesian Federation (the Caroline Islands other than Palau) attained independence in 1991. A number of internationally supervised plebiscites were held to determine whether Palau should enter into a Compact of Free Association with the United States. These have always shown a majority in favour of the proposed status, but not the 75 per cent required by the constitution.

The UN Charter, in addition to the trusteeship provisions, includes a declaration by states which 'have or assume responsibilities for the administration of territories whose peoples have not yet attained a full measure of self-government' (Art. 73(e)). The declaration is based on two principles: first, that the interests of the inhabitants of non-self-governing territories are paramount; secondly, 'the general principle of good neighbourliness, due account being taken of the interests and well-being of the rest of the world'. Members administering non-self-governing territories undertook to supply to the Secretary-General 'for information purposes . . . statistical and other information of a technical nature relating to economic, social, and educational conditions in the territories for which they are respectively responsible'.

A declaration of intent to supply the Secretary-General with technical information regarding non-self-governing territories might not seem very far-reaching, but the Secretary-General and his staff had to decide in the early days whether any use should be made of this information. It is beyond doubt that UN officials had a clear perception of future trends regarding colonial affairs, and they initiated or supported efforts by which the declaration in Article 73 of the Charter regarding the transmission of information provided the basis for a committee of the General Assembly to examine the information. The membership of the Committee on Information (as it came to be called) was divided equally between colonial and non-colonial powers, as was originally intended for the Trusteeship Council.

The responses by colonial powers to the pressure exerted through the Committee on Information varied. Australia, Britain, the Netherlands, New Zealand and the United States, while by no means enthusiastic, were willing to cooperate with the Committee on Information. Denmark also cooperated while Greenland was not fully self-governing. Belgium cooperated originally but later became recalcitrant. France initially supplied information on 16 territories, but later decided that the measure of self-government which had been granted to these territories placed them outside the scope of Article 73(e), except for the New Hebrides, which was an Anglo-French condominium and attained independence as Vanuatu in 1980. Spain transmitted information on certain territories, but Portugal consistently refused to cooperate with the UN's work on decolonization until after the coup in 1974, by which time the Committee on Information had ceased to exist.

After 1960 the main anti-colonial thrust took place in the context of the General Assembly's declaration on decolonization. Much of the declaration had expressed unexceptionable sentiments, and no votes were cast against it. But the inclusion of a paragraph stating without qualification that inadequate preparedness should never serve as a pretext for delaying independence, inevitably caused the major colonial powers to abstain on the vote. A year later, the Assembly, having rejected a Soviet proposal for a committee to ensure the liquidation of colonialism by the end of 1962, created a Special Committee to examine the implementation of the 1960 declaration. This new body had an anti-colonial majority and evoked minimal cooperation from the administering powers. In 1963 the Special Committee took over the work of the Committee on Information.

The UN Secretariat now drafts a report each year on territories within the purview of the Special Committee, and this forms the basis of the Committee's deliberations and any recommendations for the approval of the General Assembly.

Until the mid-1960s the colonial powers had tried to confine UN debate and recommendations to non-political matters, pointing out that the obligation to transmit 'statistical and other information of a technical nature' under Article 73(e) of the Charter was confined to 'economic, social, and educational conditions'; but the borderline between the political and the non-political is usually fuzzy. Social conditions in the UN system include human rights, and the administering powers were under an obligation to supply information on social conditions. It is hardly surprising that the Special Committee has often focused on politics.

While work on decolonization and on drafting the UN Covenants on human rights was proceeding, other treaties on human rights were being prepared either by the UN or one of the specialized agencies or by one of the regional agencies (see Table 6.1). Most of the treaties in the Table fall into one of three groups: those concerned with political rights and anti-discrimination measures (nos 6, 9, 10, 16, 23, 24, 28), those concerned with economic and social goals (nos 2, 4, 7, 14, 15, 17, 20, 21, 22, 25, 27, 29), and those protecting the rights of disadvantaged peoples (nos 1, 5, 8, 11, 12, 18). Of the others, three are worthy of special note: the Genocide Convention (no. 3), the Convention on the Nationality of Married Women (no. 13), and the Convention against Torture (no. 30).

7 Has the UN a Future?

We have not, in the earlier chapters, dealt with criticisms now voiced about the political role of the United Nations, except incidentally. But the UN has faults, like any human institution. Are these faults those one would expect to find in a large and complex multi-purpose intergovernmental organization at the end of its fifth decade, or are they faults which could have been prevented if only the states of which the UN is composed had been more altruistic or more far-sighted?

The first thing to be said is that the operations of the United Nations reflect the world as it is, not the world as the authors or the reader might like it to be. It is composed of 184 states, large and small, greedy and generous, allied and neutral, democratic and tyrannical, arrogant and diffident. But because the UN is one instrument for bringing into being the world as idealists would like it to be, it evokes the support of visionaries, and visionaries too often turn a blind eye to the UN's palpable faults. Former US Secretary of State George Shultz, commenting on the UN in 1985, said that it is difficult for human beings to set lofty goals and work hard for them, while recognizing that they may never be fully realized.

One criticism of the UN that is particularly made by developing countries is that its policymaking organs operate in accordance with double standards. In any UN debate about Israel, for example, it is certain that virulent denunciations will be made by delegates from countries with dismal domestic records regarding human rights. Some of the members of the Security Council who voted for Resolution 799, criticizing Israel's expulsion of Palestinians, have shown little respect for human rights at home. It is tempting to accuse these delegates of hypocrisy, but this does not help to improve the situation in the countries being criticized. Hypocrisy has, however, two undesirable effects: it brings the UN system into disrepute, and it enables those being criticized to dismiss the decisions of the UN's policymaking organs as beneath contempt. One of us remembers an Asian delegate who despaired of his own country ever putting its house in order, saying that the one thing he could do towards a better world was to vote at the UN in favour of Algerian independence. We all find it easier to solve other people's problems.

The UN, in other words, provides a convenient alibi, a diversion. There have been countless cases where delegates, ashamed of some national or regional misdemeanour, have used the UN to direct the world's attention elsewhere or where states guilty of internal repression or external aggression have taken an initiative at the UN in favour of some desirable goal such as the ending of colonialism or the renunciation of force. It is hardly surprising that these initiatives are received with scepticism if the initiating state fails to comply with the standards it advocates for others.

A second complaint is that too many resolutions of policymaking organs are irresponsible because the sponsors and supporters know that the decisions have no chance of being taken seriously.

One cannot blame states for wanting, on occasion, to change the General Assembly from a forum into a battlefield. Weak states realize that the General Assembly is the one place where all are equal, where one-state-one-vote is the norm. This situation places an obligation on the weak to temper their idealism with realism. To win a UN vote does not necessarily bring nearer the aspiration contained in the resolution.

It is fatally easy to vote for resolutions asking other nations to do something: to be more generous, more humane, less aggressive. What would be the point of voting against such proposals? But if one examines the resolutions of the General Assembly or the Economic and Social Council, and their subsidiary organs, one is struck by the large number requesting the few to do more to help the many.

One factor that lies behind the complaints already mentioned is, as suggested in Chapter 1, the disparity in UN organs between votes and effective power. Why should San Marino (population 24 000) have the same voting power in the General Assembly as China (population over one billion)?

It has for long been an accepted principle of international affairs that the basic unit is the state, whatever its size or power. The United Nations is an organization of states, and each Member has one vote. There has, however, been a growing disparity between votes and power since 1945 because of the tendency since the United Nations was founded for states with small populations to seek UN membership. The fact is that the new states have on the whole less power and fewer resources than the older ones.

This situation has led to proposals in some circles for weighted voting so that the states of which much is asked should have more votes than those on the receiving end. Weighted voting would require an amendment to the Charter, and we do not consider such a radical proposition to be practicable at the present time.

A related idea is to have a two-chamber General Assembly, one chamber composed of states (as at present) and one elected by the people world-wide. This is an attractive idea at first glance, but the second Assembly would be a mere talking-shop, since the resources to implement decisions are at the disposal of states.

Another complaint, made by professional diplomats rather than members of the general public, is of the futile nature of much UN debating. There are some political issues that have been before UN organs for more than 40 years. By now, there is little fresh to say about these issues, so that UN debates are bound to be repetitive.

The 1993 session of the General Assembly, for example, included on its agenda no fewer than seven items on the Arab–Israeli conflict.

The only way to avoid repetitious debate would be by (1) an agreement not to debate every issue every year,

(2) an agreement to set time-limits for debating hardy annuals (a guillotine or closure), or (3) a new rule of procedure or a self-denying ordinance to preclude vain repetition in individual speeches.

A final criticism which is directed against the UN is of the politicization of the Secretariat. The intention of the founders was that the staff should reach the highest standards of efficiency, competence and integrity, and should at all times be impartial, independent and international, responsible only to the United Nations: due regard was also to be paid to recruiting on as wide a geographical basis as possible (Arts. 100 and 101). The original staff were recruited at the end of the Second World War, largely from Western countries. Many of these men and women were idealists, horrified by the suffering caused by war, excited by the possibility of sharing in a bold international experiment, and relatively unconcerned with salary scales, tax-free allowances, or international perks. Sir Brian Urquhart, who served in the UN Secretariat from the start, has written that

> it is hard to recapture the freshness and enthusiasm of those pioneering days. . . . To work for peace was a dream fulfilled. . . . Bureaucracy, frustration, routine, empty rhetoric, political pettiness, and disillusionment were still in the future.

As the Secretariat has expanded and the original staff have reached pensionable age, new staff have been recruited from the parts of the world which were not adequately represented in the early days (see Appendix 2, column 5). Many UN officials are now seconded from national civil services for short-term work, often for about two years. Many of them (and their families) encounter difficulties in adjusting to life in New York or Geneva, they have to undertake unfamiliar tasks in a foreign language, and they are looking over their shoulders all the time because they expect to return to their own governmental services when their secondment to the UN is over.

In addition to the special problems of an intergovernmental agency, the Secretariat suffers from many of the defects of large organizations: private empires, time-consuming rules, useless projects, duplication of effort. Sir Brian Urquhart has commented:

> Over the years there had been a serious erosion of the standards of international civil service which we had so jealously guarded at the beginning. Too many top-level officials, political appointments, rotten boroughs, and pointless programs had rendered the Secretariat fat and flabby over the years, and it clearly needed drastic rehabilitation.

Some of these problems are gradually being exposed by various UN review bodies, but some are an inevitable consequence of thoughtless decisions by the policymaking organs.

The concept of a professional career service of international officials should not be abandoned, but this will require great firmness on the part of Secretaries-General and their directors of personnel, and much more restraint on the part of governments and ambassadors than has been evident in recent decades. If a determined effort were made, the proportion of short-term staff could be significantly reduced under a strong Secretary-General.

It is striking that none of the complaints about the UN which we have referred to in this and previous chapters (double standards, irresponsible decisions, bloc voting, disparity between votes and power, repetitious debate, politicization of the Secretariat) arise from defects in the Charter. It is true that the Charter is imperfect, reflecting the expectations of the founders half a century ago. It would certainly be possible to tidy up the Charter, eliminating a redundant phrase here or clarifying an ambiguous provision there. It is not necessary in 1994 to refer in slightly contemptuous language to 'any state which during the Second World War has been an enemy of any signatory of the present Charter' (Articles 53 and 107). It would be possible to clarify the distinction between 'affirmative' and 'concurring' votes in the Security Council (Art. 27), to make more rigid or more flexible the provision designed to prevent the General Assembly and the Security Council from dealing simultaneously with the same matters (Art. 12), to delete the provision for convening a conference to review the Charter after the tenth annual session of the General Assembly, which was held more than 30 years ago (Art. 109(3)). But the main features of the Charter which give rise to complaint, such as the veto in the Security Council (Art. 27(3)), the Council's permanent membership (Art. 23(1)), or the ban on intervening in matters of domestic jurisdiction (Art. 2(7)), probably cannot in present circumstances be amended because at least one of the veto-wielding permanent members of the Security Council would not all agree to any conceivable change.

Although the Charter declares that 'sovereign equality' is one of the principles on which the United Nations is based (Art. 2(1)), an outstanding fact about the United Nations system is that Members assume obligations which may, in certain circumstances, limit their freedom of action, and UN obligations are said to prevail over other international obligations (Art. 103). Countries which prefer not to accept such far-reaching obligations should not join the Organization.

Moreover, it is not simply that a state knows when joining exactly what the obligations of Membership will be, for the obligations can be extended later. If two-thirds of the Members, including the five permanent members of the Security Council, decide to change the Charter in a way that increases the obligations or reduces the privileges of Membership, such a change is binding on all, including states which oppose the change. It may not even be possible, in such circumstances, to resign from the United Nations because there are no provisions in the Charter for termination of Membership, other than expulsion for persistent violations of the principles of the Charter (Art. 6). Indonesia withdrew from the UN for more than a year in the 1960s, and South Africa did not for a time pay its dues or participate in most UN activities, but neither country has been able to resign its UN Membership and the consequent obligations under international law.

It is significant that almost all of the unofficial proposals to amend the Charter envisage some diminution of the sovereignty of states. There have been proposals to reduce or eliminate the right of veto by the permanent members of the Security Council, particularly in regard to the peaceful settlement of disputes; to make it obligatory for Members to comply with some or all decisions of the General Assembly; to increase the functions and powers of the United Nations regarding human rights; to provide for the compulsory jurisdiction of the International Court. Those are no doubt pointers for the future, but the time has not yet arrived for world government.

All the same, the world has entered an era in which all states accept a diminution of sovereignty, in exchange for a part-share in the sovereignty of all other states. Only Switzerland, of the world's independent states, prefers to remain aloof. In 1960, when UN Membership stood at 99, the UN Secretariat proposed adapting the Headquarters building for a possible Membership of 'some 120 . . . within a not too distant future'. This number was, in fact, reached in 1966 (see Table 1.1). UN membership now stands at 184.

The more than trebling of UN Membership from the original 51 undoubtedly means that everything takes longer, but a more significant change, as has been stressed in Chapters 1 and 3, is in the focus and character of UN debates and decisions. Many of the new states share some common characteristics: most are relatively underdeveloped, dependent on a single or very few exports, only recently freed from foreign rule, and sensitive about perceived racial slights. Many find it impossible to keep up interest payments on national debts, and many believe that international trade operates to their disadvantage. They may be struggling to develop or sustain democratic institutions for partly illiterate populations, but they are indifferent to military alignments, hoping to maintain their own security through neutrality. When Cold War issues arose at the United Nations, their inclination was to cry 'a plague on both your houses'.

It is already the case that the United Nations has been much more active in promoting economic and social advancement than was envisaged when the Organization was founded. Yet there is a disappointing aspect to all this activity, because the absolute gap between per capita incomes of rich and poor countries has been progressively widening. This gap cannot be narrowed until the developing countries achieve a substantially higher rate of environmentally sustainable economic growth. Much suffering could be avoided if only the resources of the earth and the skill of the human brain and hand were used more rationally.

Economic and social instability can have international political repercussions. Many of the political problems with which the United Nations has been confronted could have been eased, if not entirely avoided, if only economic and social measures had been applied early enough and on a sufficient scale. The United Nations should not be blamed for international crises, any more than we blame lifeboat crews for shipwrecks or fire-brigades for arson.

It is sometimes said that, while the UN has had a disappointing political record, it has many economic and social achievements to its credit. This may be true, but governments and people will not support indefinitely an organization that is manifestly failing in its primary purposes: 'to save succeeding generations from the scourge of war', to pursue 'justice and respect' for international obligations, to enable ordinary people 'to practise tolerance and live together in peace with one another as good neighbours', to ensure that armed force is not used except 'in the common interest' (Preamble to the Charter).

With all its faults, the United Nations provides a framework for bilateral or multilateral negotiations, and UN officials and fair-minded diplomats can facilitate understanding or agreement by behind-the-scenes activities. It is difficult to assess, and impossible to document, the value of initiatives of this kind: success must usually be anonymous. The authors of this book know of cases where uncommitted diplomats, impartial officials, or representatives of non-governmental organizations have played a crucial role when things got difficult, as Norway did regarding the Israel–Palestine problem. This moderating function is often exercised quietly in the lobbies rather than publicly in the meetings.

The United Nations is an essential forum for multilateral diplomacy. For small states with limited resources for maintaining diplomatic missions, the UN is the one place where it is possible to relate to all other states as well as to liberation movements, specialized agencies, and regional bodies. There is no better place to learn the uses and abuses of the diplomatic method.

There is often an element of gamesmanship in international negotiation. If agreement depends on mutual concessions, as is almost always the case, it is not surprising that the parties should hold possible concessions in reserve, which can later be abandoned with safety. Negotiation, when it is real, involves a search to discover what there is in the position of the other party which cannot be bargained away. This is inevitably a lengthy process.

It is easy to become impatient about long-drawn-out negotiations over such questions as disarmament. If one mistrusts the intentions of one side or the other and therefore believes that negotiations are doomed to failure, or if one believes that disarmament is more likely to be achieved by unilateral initiative than by international agreement, the spectacle of intermittent negotiation year after year confirms one's initial scepticism. There are, however, two main reasons why the attempt to negotiate should not be abandoned. The first is that one can never be absolutely certain that the efforts will not ultimately be successful, as happened in the case of chemical weapons: it is a poor excuse to give up the attempt on the ground that the other side may be insincere. The second reason for persisting is that the actual process of negotiation, even if it is inconclusive, can help to increase mutual understanding and reduce tension.

'Has the UN a future?' is an unreal question. The UN is there, and it will continue to be there. If the UN did not exist, it would be necessary to invent it. The question is not whether the UN has a future, but rather how it can be strengthened and made more effective.

The United Nations belongs to all the Members. It is not a panacea but, in the words of Ernest Gross, 'a set of rules and a set of tools'. The rules are contained in or derived from the Charter and are binding: the tools must be fashioned and adapted for each job when the precise needs are known. The notion of an international interest may sometimes seem an elusive abstraction, but its pursuit cannot ultimately be contrary to the real interests of any state.

The United Nations does not end the need for wisdom. The United Nations is an instrument at the disposal of states, to be used or misused or ignored. 'As long as there are men', Dag Hammarskjöld once said, 'they will quarrel; as long as there are nations, they will have conflicts . . . I believe that conflicts may always lead to open strife, an open clash. Under such circumstances and not knowing how far such a clash may lead, I think there is plenty to do for an Organization like the United Nations.'

Appendix 1
Charter of the United Nations and Statute of the International Court of Justice

Introductory Note

The Charter of the United Nations was signed on 26 June 1945, in San Francisco, at the conclusion of the United Nations Conference on International Organization, and came into force on 24 October 1945. The Statute of the International Court of Justice is an integral part of the Charter.

Amendments to Articles 23, 27 and 61 of the Charter were adopted by the General Assembly on 17 December 1963 and came into force on 31 August 1965. A further amendment to Article 61 was adopted by the General Assembly on 20 December 1971, and came into force on 24 September 1973. An amendment to Article 109, adopted by the General Assembly on 20 December 1965, came into force on 12 June 1968.

The amendment to Article 23 enlarges the membership of the Security Council from eleven to fifteen. The amended Article 27 provides that decisions of the Security Council on procedural matters shall be made by an affirmative vote of nine members (formerly seven) and on all other matters by an affirmative vote of nine members (formerly seven), including the concurring votes of the five permanent members of the Security Council.

The amendment to Article 61, which entered into force on 31 August 1965, enlarged the membership of the Economic and Social Council from eighteen to twenty-seven. The subsequent amendment to that Article, which entered into force on 24 September 1973, further increased the membership of the Council from twenty-seven to fifty-four.

The amendment to Article 109, which relates to the first paragraph of that Article, provides that a General Conference of Member States for the purpose of reviewing the Charter may be held at

113

a date and place to be fixed by a two-thirds vote of the members of the General Assembly and by a vote of any nine members (formerly seven) of the Security Council. Paragraph 3 of Article 109, which deals with the consideration of a possible review conference during the tenth regular session of the General Assembly, has been retained in its original form in its reference to a 'vote, of any seven members of the Security Council', the paragraph having been acted upon in 1955 by the General Assembly, at its tenth regular session, and by the Security Council.

CHARTER OF THE UNITED NATIONS

WE THE PEOPLES
OF THE UNITED NATIONS
DETERMINED

> to save succeeding generations from the scourge of war, which twice in our life-time has brought untold sorrow to mankind, and

> to reaffirm faith in fundamental human rights, in the dignity and worth of the human person, in the equal rights of men and women and of nations large and small, and

> to establish conditions under which justice and respect for the obligations arising from treaties and other sources of international law can be maintained, and

> to promote social progress and better standards of life in larger freedom,

AND FOR THESE ENDS

> to practice tolerance and live together in peace with one another as good neighbours, and

> to unite our strength to maintain international peace and security, and

> to ensure, by the acceptance of principles and the institution of methods, that armed force shall not be used, save in the common interest, and

> to employ international machinery for the promotion of the economic and social advancement of all peoples,

HAVE RESOLVED TO COMBINE OUR EFFORTS TO ACCOMPLISH THESE AIMS

> Accordingly, our respective Governments, through representatives assembled in the city of San Francisco, who have exhibited their full powers found to be in good and due form, have agreed to

the present Charter of the United Nations and do hereby establish an international organization to be known as the United Nations.

CHAPTER I

PURPOSES AND PRINCIPLES

Article 1

The Purposes of the United Nations are:

1. To maintain international peace and security, and to that end: to take effective collective measures for the prevention and removal of threats to the peace, and for the suppression of acts of aggression or other breaches of the peace, and to bring about by peaceful means, and in conformity with the principles of justice and international law, adjustment or settlement of international disputes or situations which might lead to a breach of the peace;

2. To develop friendly relations among nations based on respect for the principle of equal rights and self-determination of peoples, and to take other appropriate measures to strengthen universal peace;

3. To achieve international co-operation in solving international problems of an economic, social, cultural, or humanitarian character, and in promoting and encouraging respect for human rights and for fundamental freedoms for all without distinction as to race, sex, language, or religion; and

4. To be a centre for harmonizing the actions of nations in the attainment of these common ends.

Article 2

The Organization and its Members, in pursuit of the Purposes stated in Article 1, shall act in accordance with the following Principles.

1. The Organization is based on the principle of the sovereign equality of all its Members.

2. All Members, in order to ensure to all of them the rights and benefits resulting from membership, shall fulfil in good faith the obligations assumed by them in accordance with the present Charter.

3. All Members shall settle their international disputes by peaceful means in such a manner that international peace and security, and justice, are not endangered.

4. All Members shall refrain in their international relations from the threat or use of force against the territorial integrity or political independence of any state, or in any other manner inconsistent with the Purposes of the United Nations.

5. All Members shall give the United Nations every assistance in any action it takes in accordance with the present Charter, and shall refrain from giving assistance to any state against which the United Nations is taking preventive or enforcement action.

6. The Organization shall ensure that states which are not Members of the United Nations act in accordance with these Principles so far as may be necessary for the maintenance of international peace and security.

7. Nothing contained in the present Charter shall authorize the United Nations to intervene in matters which are essentially within the domestic jurisdiction of any state or shall require the Members to submit such matters to settlement under the present Charter; but this principle shall not prejudice the application of enforcement measures under Chapter VII.

CHAPTER II

MEMBERSHIP

Article 3

The original Members of the United Nations shall be the states which, having participated in the United Nations Conference on International Organization at San Francisco, or having previously signed the Declaration by United Nations of 1 January 1942, sign the present Charter and ratify it in accordance with Article 110.

Article 4

1. Membership in the United Nations is open to all other peace-loving states which accept the obligations contained in the present Charter and, in the judgment of the Organization, are able and willing to carry out these obligations.

2. The admission of any such state to membership in the United Nations will be effected by a decision of the General Assembly upon the recommendation of the Security Council.

Article 5

A Member of the United Nations against which preventive or enforcement action has been taken by the Security Council may be suspended from the exercise of the rights and privileges of membership by the General Assembly upon the recommendation of the Security Council. The exercise of these rights and privileges may be restored by the Security Council.

Article 6

A Member of the United Nations which has persistently violated the Principles contained in the present Charter may be expelled from the Organization by the General Assembly upon the recommendation of the Security Council.

CHAPTER III

ORGANS

Article 7

1. There are established as the principal organs of the United Nations: a General Assembly, a Security Council, an Economic and Social Council, a Trusteeship Council, an International Court of Justice, and a Secretariat.

2. Such subsidiary organs as may be found necessary may be established in accordance with the present Charter.

Article 8

The United Nations shall place no restrictions on the eligibility of men and women to participate in any capacity and under conditions of equality in its principal and subsidiary organs.

CHAPTER IV

THE GENERAL ASSEMBLY

Composition

Article 9

1. The General Assembly shall consist of all the Members of the United Nations.

2. Each Member shall have not more than five representatives in the General Assembly.

Functions and Powers

Article 10

The General Assembly may discuss any questions or any matters within the scope of the present Charter or relating to the powers and functions of any organs provided for in the present Charter, and, except as provided in Article 12, may make recommendations to the Members of the United Nations or to the Security Council or to both on any such questions or matters.

Article 11

1. The General Assembly may consider the general principles of co-operation in the maintenance of international peace and security, including the principles governing disarmament and the regulation of armaments, and may make recommendations with regard to such principles to the Members or to the Security Council or to both.

2. The General Assembly may discuss any questions relating to the maintenance of international peace and security brought before

it by any Member of the United Nations, or by the Security Council, or by a state which is not a Member of the United Nations in accordance with Article 35, paragraph 2, and, except as provided in Article 12, may make recommendations with regard to any such questions to the state or states concerned or to the Security Council or to both. Any such question on which action is necessary shall be referred to the Security Council by the General Assembly either before or after discussion.

3. The General Assembly may call the attention of the Security Council to situations which are likely to endanger international peace and security.

4. The powers of the General Assembly set forth in this Article shall not limit the general scope of Article 10.

Article 12

1. While the Security Council is exercising in respect of any dispute or situation the functions assigned to it in the present Charter, the General Assembly shall not make any recommendation with regard to that dispute or situation unless the Security Council so requests.

2. The Secretary-General, with the consent of the Security Council, shall notify the General Assembly at each session of any matters relative to the maintenance of international peace and security which are being dealt with by the Security Council and shall similarly notify the General Assembly, or the Members of the United Nations if the General Assembly is not in session, immediately the Security Council ceases to deal with such matters.

Article 13

1. The General Assembly shall initiate studies and make recommendations for the purpose of:

a. promoting international co-operation in the political field and encouraging the progressive development of international law and its codification;

b. promoting international co-operation in the economic, social, cultural, educational, and health fields, and assisting in the realization of human rights and fundamental freedoms for all without distinction as to race, sex, language, or religion.

2. The further responsibilities, functions and powers of the General Assembly with respect to matters mentioned in paragraph 1(b) above are set forth in Chapters IX and X.

Article 14

Subject to the provisions of Article 12, the General Assembly may recommend measures for the peaceful adjustment of any situation, regardless of origin, which it deems likely to impair the general welfare or friendly relations among nations, including situations resulting from a violation of the provisions of the present Charter setting forth the Purposes and Principles of the United Nations.

Article 15

1. The General Assembly shall receive and consider annual and special reports from the Security Council; these reports shall include an account of the measures that the Security Council has decided upon or taken to maintain international peace and security.

2. The General Assembly shall receive and consider reports from the other organs of the United Nations.

Article 16

The General Assembly shall perform such functions with respect to the international trusteeship system as are assigned to it under Chapters XII and XIII, including the approval of the trusteeship agreements for areas not designated as strategic.

Article 17

1. The General Assembly shall consider and approve the budget of the Organization.

2. The expenses of the Organization shall be borne by the Members as apportioned by the General Assembly.

3. The General Assembly shall consider and approve any financial and budgetary arrangements with specialized agencies referred to in Article 57 and shall examine the administrative budgets of such specialized agencies with a view to making recommendations to the agencies concerned.

Voting

Article 18

1. Each member of the General Assembly shall have one vote.

2. Decisions of the General Assembly on important questions shall be made by a two-thirds majority of the members present and voting. These questions shall include: recommendations with respect to the maintenance of international peace and security, the election of the non-permanent members of the Security Council, the election of the members of the Economic and Social Council, the election of members of the Trusteeship Council in accordance with paragraph 1(c) of Article 86, the admission of new Members to the United Nations, the suspension of the rights and privileges of membership, the expulsion of Members, questions relating to the operation of the trusteeship system, and budgetary questions.

3. Decisions on other questions, including the determination of additional categories of questions to be decided by a two-thirds majority, shall be made by a majority of the members present and voting.

Article 19

A Member of the United Nations which is in arrears in the payment of its financial contributions to the Organization shall have no vote in the General Assembly if the amount of its arrears equals or exceeds the amount of the contributions due from it for the preceding two full years. The General Assembly may, nevertheless, permit such a Member to vote if it is satisfied that the failure to pay is due to conditions beyond the control of the Member.

Procedure

Article 20

The General Assembly shall meet in regular annual sessions and in such special sessions as occasion may require. Special sessions shall be convoked by the Secretary-General at the request of the Security Council or of a majority of the Members of the United Nations.

Article 21

The General Assembly shall adopt its own rules of procedure. It shall elect its President for each session.

Article 22

The General Assembly may establish such subsidiary organs as it deems necessary for the performance of its functions.

CHAPTER V

THE SECURITY COUNCIL

Composition

Article 23

1. The Security Council shall consist of fifteen Members of the United Nations. The Republic of China, France, the Union of Soviet Socialist Republics, the United Kingdom of Great Britain and Northern Ireland, and the United States of America shall be permanent members of the Security Council. The General Assembly shall elect ten other Members of the United Nations to be non-permanent members of the Security Council, due regard being specially paid, in the first instance to the contribution of Members of the United Nations to the maintenance of international peace and security and to the other purposes of the Organization, and also to equitable geographical distribution.

2. The non-permanent members of the Security Council shall be elected for a term of two years. In the first election of the non-permanent members after the increase of the membership of the

Security Council from eleven to fifteen, two of the four additional members shall be chosen for a term of one year. A retiring member shall not be eligible for immediate re-election.

3. Each member of the Security Council shall have one representative.

Functions and Powers

Article 24

1. In order to ensure prompt and effective action by the United Nations, its Members confer on the Security Council primary responsibility for the maintenance of international peace and security, and agree that in carrying out its duties under this responsibility the Security Council acts on their behalf.

2. In discharging these duties the Security Council shall act in accordance with the Purposes and Principles of the United Nations. The specific powers granted to the Security Council for the discharge of these duties are laid down in Chapters VI, VII, VIII, and XII.

3. The Security Council shall submit annual and, when necessary, special reports to the General Assembly for its consideration.

Article 25

The Members of the United Nations agree to accept and carry out the decisions of the Security Council in accordance with the present Charter.

Article 26

In order to promote the establishment and maintenance of international peace and security with the least diversion for armaments of the world's human and economic resources, the Security Council shall be responsible for formulating, with the assistance of the Military Staff Committee referred to in Article 47, plans to be submitted to the Members of the United Nations for the establishment of a system for the regulation of armaments.

Voting

Article 27

1. Each member of the Security Council shall have one vote.

2. Decisions of the Security Council on procedural matters shall be made by an affirmative vote of nine members.

3. Decisions of the Security Council on all other matters shall be made by an affirmative vote of nine members including the concurring votes of the permanent members; provided that, in decisions under Chapter VI, and under paragraph 3 of Article 52, a party to a dispute shall abstain from voting.

Procedure

Article 28

1. The Security Council shall be so organized as to be able to function continuously. Each member of the Security Council shall for this purpose be represented at all times at the seat of the Organization.

2. The Security Council shall hold periodic meetings at which each of its members may, if it so desires, be represented by a member of the government or by some other specially designated representative.

3. The Security Council may hold meetings at such places other than the seat of the Organization as in its judgment will best facilitate its work.

Article 29

The Security Council may establish such subsidiary organs as it deems necessary for the performance of its functions.

Article 30

The Security Council shall adopt its own rules of procedure, including the method of selecting its President.

Article 31

Any Member of the United Nations which is not a member of the Security Council may participate, without vote, in the discussion of any question brought before the Security Council whenever the latter considers that the interests of that Member are specially affected.

Article 32

Any Member of the United Nations which is not a member of the Security Council or any state which is not a Member of the United Nations, if it is a party to a dispute under consideration by the Security Council, shall be invited to participate, without vote, in the discussion relating to the dispute. The Security Council shall lay down such conditions as it deems just for the participation of a state which is not a Member of the United Nations.

CHAPTER VI

PACIFIC SETTLEMENT OF DISPUTES

Article 33

1. The parties to any dispute, the continuance of which is likely to endanger the maintenance of international peace and security, shall, first of all, seek a solution by negotiation, enquiry, mediation, conciliation, arbitration, judicial settlement, resort to regional agencies

or arrangements, or other peaceful means of their own choice.

2. The Security Council shall, when it deems necessary, call upon the parties to settle their dispute by such means.

Article 34

The Security Council may investigate any dispute, or any situation which might lead to international friction or give rise to a dispute, in order to determine whether the continuance of the dispute or situation is likely to endanger the maintenance of international peace and security.

Article 35

1. Any Member of the United Nations may bring any dispute, or any situation of the nature referred to in Article 34, to the attention of the Security Council or of the General Assembly.

2. A state which is not a Member of the United Nations may bring to the attention of the Security Council or of the General Assembly any dispute to which it is a party if it accepts in advance, for the purposes of the dispute, the obligations of pacific settlement provided in the present Charter.

3. The proceedings of the General Assembly in respect of matters brought to its attention under this Article will be subject to the provisions of Articles 11 and 12.

Article 36

1. The Security Council may, at any stage of a dispute of the nature referred to in Article 33 or of a situation of like nature, recommend appropriate procedures or methods of adjustment.

2. The Security Council should take into consideration any procedures for the settlement of the dispute which have already been adopted by the parties.

3. In making recommendations under this Article the Security Council should also take into consideration that legal disputes should as a general rule be referred by the parties to the International Court of Justice in accordance with the provisions of the Statute of the Court.

Article 37

1. Should the parties to a dispute of the nature referred to in Article 33 fail to settle it by the means indicated in that Article, they shall refer it to the Security Council.

2. If the Security Council deems that the continuance of the dispute is in fact likely to endanger the maintenance of international peace and security, it shall decide whether to take action under Article 36 or to recommend such terms of settlement as it may consider appropriate.

Article 38

Without prejudice to the provisions of Articles 33 to 37, the Security Council may, if all the parties to any dispute so request, make recommendations to the parties with a view to a pacific settlement of the dispute.

CHAPTER VII

ACTION WITH RESPECT TO THREATS TO THE PEACE, BREACHES OF THE PEACE, AND ACTS OF AGGRESSION

Article 39

The Security Council shall determine the existence of any threat to the peace, breach of the peace, or act of aggression and shall make recommendations, or decide what measures shall be taken in accordance with Articles 41 and 42, to maintain or restore international peace and security.

Article 40

In order to prevent an aggravation of the situation, the Security Council may, before making the recommendations or deciding upon the measures provided for in Article 39, call upon the parties concerned to comply with such provisional measures as it deems necessary or desirable. Such provisional measures shall be without prejudice to the rights, claims, or position of the parties concerned. The Security Council shall duly take account of failure to comply with such provisional measures.

Article 41

The Security Council may decide what measures not involving the use of armed force are to be employed to give effect to its decisions, and it may call upon the Members of the United Nations to apply such measures. These may include complete or partial interruption of economic relations and of rail, sea, air, postal, telegraphic, radio, and other means of communication, and the severance of diplomatic relations.

Article 42

Should the Security Council consider that measures provided for in Article 41 would be inadequate or have proved to be inadequate, it may take such action by air, sea, or land forces as may be necessary to maintain or restore international peace and security. Such action may include demonstrations, blockade, and other operations by air, sea, or land forces of Members of the United Nations.

Article 43

1. All Members of the United Nations, in order to contribute to the maintenance of international peace and security, undertake to make available to the Security Council, on its call in accordance with a special agreement or agreements, armed forces, assistance, and facilities, including rights of passage, necessary for the purpose of maintaining international peace and security.

2. Such agreement or agreements shall govern the numbers and types of forces, their degree of readiness and general location, and the nature of the facilities and assistance to be provided.

3. The agreement or agreements shall be negotiated as soon as possible on the initiative of the Security Council. They shall be concluded between the Security Council and Members or between the Security Council and groups of Members and shall be subject to ratification by the signatory states in accordance with their respective constitutional processes.

Article 44

When the Security Council has decided to use force it shall, before calling upon a Member not represented on it to provide armed forces in fulfilment of the obligations assumed under Article 43, invite that Member, if the Member so desires, to participate in the decisions of the Security Council concerning the employment of contingents of that Member's armed forces.

Article 45

In order to enable the United Nations to take urgent military measures, Members shall hold immediately available national airforce contingents for combined international enforcement action. The strength and degree of readiness of these contingents and plans for their combined action shall be determined, within the limits laid down in the special agreement or agreements referred to in Article 43, by the Security Council with assistance of the Military Staff Committee.

Article 46

Plans for the application of armed force shall be made by the Security Council with the assistance of the Military Staff Committee.

Article 47

1. There shall be established a Military Staff Committee to advise and assist the Security Council on all questions relating to the Security Council's military requirements for the maintenance of international peace and security, the employment and command of forces placed at its disposal, the regulation of armaments, and possible disarmament.

2. The Military Staff Committee shall consist of the Chiefs of Staff of the permanent members of the Security Council or their representatives. Any Members of the United Nations not permanently represented on the Committee shall be invited by the Committee to be associated with it when the efficient discharge of the Committee's responsibilities requires the participation of that Member in its work.

3. The Military Staff Committee shall be responsible under the Security Council for the strategic direction of any armed forces placed at the disposal of the Security Council. Questions relating to the command of such forces shall be worked out subsequently.

4. The Military Staff Committee, with the authorization of the Security Council and after consultation with appropriate regional agencies, may establish regional sub-committees.

Article 48

1. The action required to carry out the decisions of the Security Council for the maintenance of international peace and security shall be taken by all the Members of the United Nations or by some of them, as the Security Council may determine.

2. Such decisions shall be carried out by the Members of the United Nations directly and through their action in the appropriate international agencies of which they are members.

Article 49

The Members of the United Nations shall join in affording mutual assistance in carrying out the measures decided upon by the Security Council.

Article 50

If preventive or enforcement measures against any state are taken by the Security Council, any other state, whether a Member of the United Nations or not, which finds itself confronted with special economic problems arising from the carrying out of those measures shall have the right to consult the Security Council with regard to a solution of those problems.

Article 51

Nothing in the present Charter shall impair the inherent right of individual or collective self-defence if an armed attack occurs against a Member of the United Nations, until the Security Council has taken measures necessary to maintain international peace and security. Measures taken by Members in the exercise of this right of self-defence shall be immediately reported to the Security Council and shall not in any way affect the authority and responsibility of the Security Council under the present Charter to take at any time such action as it deems necessary in order to maintain or restore international peace and security.

CHAPTER VIII

REGIONAL ARRANGEMENTS

Article 52

1. Nothing in the present Charter precludes the existence of regional arrangements or agencies for dealing with such matters relating to the maintenance of international peace and security as are appropriate for regional action, provided that such agreements or agencies and their activities are consistent with the Purposes and Principles of the United Nations.

2. The Members of the United Nations entering into such arrangements or constituting such agencies shall make every effort to achieve pacific settlement of local disputes through such regional arrangements or by such regional agencies before referring them to the Security Council.

3. The Security Council shall encourage the development of pacific settlement of local disputes through such regional arrangements or by such regional agencies either on the initiative of the states concerned or by reference from the Security Council.

4. This Article in no way impairs the application of Articles 34 and 35.

Article 53

1. The Security Council shall, where appropriate, utilize such regional arrangements or agencies for enforcement action under its authority. But no enforcement action shall be taken under regional arrangements or by regional agencies without the authorization of the Security Council, with the exception of measures against any enemy state, as defined in paragraph 2 of this Article, provided for pursuant to Article 107 or in regional arrangements directed against renewal of aggressive policy on the part of any such state, until such time as the Organization may, on request of the Governments concerned, be charged with the responsibility for preventing further aggression by such a state.

2. The term enemy state as used in paragraph 1 of this Article applies to any state which during the Second World War has been an enemy of any signatory of the present Charter.

Article 54

The Security Council shall at all times be kept fully informed of activities undertaken or in contemplation under regional arrangements or by regional agencies for the maintenance of international peace and security.

CHAPTER IX

INTERNATIONAL ECONOMIC AND SOCIAL CO-OPERATION

Article 55

With a view to the creation of conditions of stability and well-being which are necessary for peaceful and friendly relations among nations based on respect for the principle of equal rights and self-determination of peoples, the United Nations shall promote:

    a. higher standards of living, full employment, and conditions of economic and social progress and development;

    b. solutions of international economic, social, health, and related problems; and international cultural and educational cooperation; and

    c. universal respect for, and observance of, human rights and fundamental freedoms for all without distinction as to race, sex, language, or religion.

Article 56

All Members pledge themselves to take joint and separate action in co-operation with the Organization for the achievement of the purposes set forth in Article 55.

Article 57

1. The various specialized agencies, established by intergovernmental agreement and having wide international responsibilities, as defined in their basic instruments, in economic, social, cultural, educational, health, and related fields, shall be brought into relationship with the United Nations in accordance with the provisions of Article 63.

2. Such agencies thus brought into relationship with the United Nations are hereinafter referred to as specialized agencies.

Article 58

The Organization shall make recommendations for the co-ordination of the policies and activities of the specialized agencies.

Article 59

The Organization shall, where appropriate, initiate negotiations among the states concerned for the creation of any new specialized agencies required for the accomplishment of the purposes set forth in Article 55.

Article 60

Responsibility for the discharge of the functions of the Organization set forth in this Chapter shall be vested in the General Assembly and, under the authority of the General Assembly, in the Economic and Social Council, which shall have for this purpose the powers set forth in Chapter X.

CHAPTER X

THE ECONOMIC AND SOCIAL COUNCIL

Composition

Article 61

1. The Economic and Social Council shall consist of fifty-four Members of the United Nations elected by the General Assembly.

2. Subject to the provisions of paragraph 3, eighteen members of the Economic and Social Council shall be elected each year for a term of three years. A retiring member shall be eligible for immediate re-election.

3. At the first election after the increase in the membership of the Economic and Social Council from twenty-seven to fifty-four members, in addition to the members elected in place of the nine members whose term of office expires at the end of that year, twenty-seven additional members shall be elected. Of these twenty-seven additional members, the term of office of nine members so elected shall expire at the end of one year, and of nine other members at the end of two years, in accordance with arrangements made by the General Assembly.

4. Each member of the Economic and Social Council shall have one representative.

Functions and Powers

Article 62

1. The Economic and Social Council may make or initiate studies and reports with respect to international economic, social, cultural, educational, health, and related matters and may make recommendations with respect to any such matters to the General Assembly, to the Members of the United Nations, and to the specialized agencies concerned.

2. It may make recommendations for the purpose of promoting respect for, and observance of, human rights and fundamental freedoms for all.

3. It may prepare draft conventions for submission to the General Assembly, with respect to matters falling within its competence.

4. It may call, in accordance with the rules prescribed by the United Nations, international conferences on matters falling within its competence.

Article 63

1. The Economic and Social Council may enter into agreements with any of the agencies referred to in Article 57, defining the terms on which the agency concerned shall be brought into relationship with the United Nations. Such agreements shall be subject to approval by the General Assembly.

2. It may co-ordinate the activities of the specialized agencies through consultation with and recommendations to such agencies and through recommendations to the General Assembly and to the Members of the United Nations.

Article 64

1. The Economic and Social Council may take appropriate steps to obtain regular reports from the specialized agencies. It may make arrangements with the Members of the United Nations and with the specialized agencies to obtain reports on the steps taken to give effect to its own recommendations and to recommendations on matters falling within its competence made by the General Assembly.

2. It may communicate its observations on these reports to the General Assembly.

Article 65

The Economic and Social Council may furnish information to the Security Council and shall assist the Security Council upon its request.

Article 66

1. The Economic and Social Council shall perform such functions as fall within its competence in connexion with the carrying out of the recommendations of the General Assembly.

2. It may, with the approval of the General Assembly, perform services at the request of Members of the United Nations and at the request of specialized agencies.

3. It shall perform such other functions as are specified elsewhere in the present Charter or as may be assigned to it by the General Assembly.

Voting

Article 67

1. Each member of the Economic and Social Council shall have one vote.

2. Decisions of the Economic and Social Council shall be made by a majority of the members present and voting.

Procedure

Article 68

The Economic and Social Council shall set up commissions in economic and social fields and for the promotion of human rights, and such other commissions as may be required for the performance of its functions.

Article 69

The Economic and Social Council shall invite any Member of the United Nations to participate, without vote, in its deliberations on any matter of particular concern to that Member.

Article 70

The Economic and Social Council may make arrangements for representatives of the specialized agencies to participate, without vote, in its deliberations and in those of the commissions established by it, and for its representatives to participate in the deliberations of the specialized agencies.

Article 71

The Economic and Social Council may make suitable arrangements for consultation with non-governmental organizations which are concerned with matters within its competence. Such arrangements may be made with international organizations and, where appropriate, with national organizations after consultation with the Member of the United Nations concerned.

Article 72

1. The Economic and Social Council shall adopt its own rules of procedure, including the method of selecting its President.
2. The Economic and Social Council shall meet as required in accordance with its rules, which shall include provision for the convening of meetings on the request of a majority of its members.

CHAPTER XI

DECLARATION REGARDING NON-SELF-GOVERNING TERRITORIES

Article 73

Members of the United Nations which have or assume responsibilities for the administration of territories whose peoples have not yet attained a full measure of self-government recognize the principle that the interests of the inhabitants of these territories are paramount, and accept as a sacred trust the obligation to promote to the utmost, within the system of international peace and security established by the present Charter, the well-being of the inhabitants of these territories, and, to this end:

a. to ensure, with due respect for the culture of the peoples concerned, their political, economic, social, and educational advancement, their just treatment, and their protection against abuses;

b. to develop self-government, to take due account of the political aspirations of the peoples, and to assist them in the progressive development of their free political institutions, according to the particular circumstances of each territory and its peoples and their varying stages of advancement;

c. to further international peace and security;

d. to promote constructive measures of development, to encourage research, and to co-operate with one another and, when and where appropriate, with specialized international bodies with a view to the practical achievement of the social, economic, and scientific purposes set forth in this Article; and

e. to transmit regularly to the Secretary-General for information purposes, subject to such limitation as security and constitutional considerations may require, statistical and other information of a technical nature relating to economic, social, and educational conditions in the territories for which they are respectively responsible other than those territories to which Chapters XII and XIII apply.

Article 74

Members of the United Nations also agree that their policy in respect of the territories to which this Chapter applies, no less than in respect of their metropolitan areas, must be based on the general principle of good-neighbourliness, due account being taken of the interests and well-being of the rest of the world, in social, economic, and commercial matters.

CHAPTER XII

INTERNATIONAL TRUSTEESHIP SYSTEM

Article 75

The United Nations shall establish under its authority an international trusteeship system for the administration and supervision of such territories as may be placed there-under by subsequent individual agreements. These territories are hereinafter referred to as trust territories.

Article 76

The basic objectives of the trusteeship system, in accordance with the Purposes of the United Nations laid down in Article 1 of the present Charter, shall be:

a. to further international peace and security;

b. to promote the political, economic, social, and educational advancement of the inhabitants of the trust territories, and their progressive development towards self-government or independence as may be appropriate to the particular circumstances of each territory and its peoples and the freely expressed wishes of the peoples concerned, and as may be provided by the terms of each trusteeship agreement;

c. to encourage respect for human rights and for fundamental freedoms for all without distinction as to race, sex, language, or religion, and to encourage recognition of the interdependence of the peoples of the world; and

d. to ensure equal treatment in social, economic, and commercial matters for all Members of the United Nations and their nationals, and also equal treatment for the latter in the administration of justice, without prejudice to the attainment of the foregoing objectives and subject to the provisions of Article 80.

Article 77

1. The trusteeship system shall apply to such territories in the following categories as may be placed thereunder by means of trusteeship agreements:

a. territories now held under mandate;

b. territories which may be detached from enemy states as a result of the Second World War; and

c. territories voluntarily placed under the system by states responsible for their administration.

2. It will be a matter for subsequent agreement as to which territories in the foregoing categories will be brought under the trusteeship system and upon what terms.

Article 78

The trusteeship system shall not apply to territories which have become Members of the United Nations, relationship among which shall be based on respect for the principle of sovereign equality.

Article 79

The terms of trusteeship for each territory to be placed under the trusteeship system, including any alteration or amendment, shall be agreed upon by the states directly concerned, including the mandatory power in the case of territories held under mandate by a Member of the United Nations, and shall be approved as provided for in Articles 83 and 85.

Article 80

1. Except as may be agreed upon in individual trusteeship agreements, made under Articles 77, 79, and 81, placing each territory under the trusteeship system, and until such agreements have been concluded, nothing in this Chapter shall be construed in or of itself to alter in any manner the rights whatsoever of any states or any peoples or the terms of existing international instruments to which Members of the United Nations may respectively be parties.

2. Paragraph 1 of this Article shall not be interpreted as giving grounds for delay or postponement of the negotiation and conclusion of agreements for placing mandated and other territories under the trusteeship system as provided for in Article 77.

Article 81

The trusteeship agreement shall in each case include the terms under which the trust territory will be administered and designate the authority which will exercise the administration of the trust territory. Such authority, hereinafter called the administering authority, may be one or more states or the Organization itself.

Article 82

There may be designated, in any trusteeship agreement, a strategic area or areas which may include part or all of the trust territory to which the agreement applies, without prejudice to any special agreement or agreements made under Article 43.

Article 83

1. All functions of the United Nations relating to strategic areas, including the approval of the terms of the trusteeship agreements and of their alteration or amendment, shall be exercised by the Security Council.

2. The basic objectives set forth in Article 76 shall be applicable to the people of each strategic area.

3. The Security Council shall, subject to the provisions of the trusteeship agreements and without prejudice to security considerations, avail itself of the assistance of the Trusteeship Council to perform those functions of the United Nations under the trusteeship system relating to political, economic, social, and educational matters in the strategic areas.

Article 84

It shall be the duty of the administering authority to ensure that the trust territory shall play its part in the maintenance of international peace and security. To this end the administering authority may make use of volunteer forces, facilities, and assistance from the trust territory in carrying out the obligations towards the Security

Council undertaken in this regard by the administering authority, as well as for local defence and the maintenance of law and order within the trust territory.

Article 85

1. The functions of the United Nations with regard to trusteeship agreements for all areas not designated as strategic, including the approval of the terms of the trusteeship agreements and of their alteration or amendment, shall be exercised by the General Assembly.

2. The Trusteeship Council, operating under the authority of the General Assembly, shall assist the General Assembly in carrying out these functions.

CHAPTER XIII

THE TRUSTEESHIP COUNCIL

Composition

Article 86

1. The Trusteeship Council shall consist of the following Members of the United Nations:

    a. those Members administering trust territories;

    b. such of those Members mentioned by name in Article 23 as are not administering trust territories; and

    c. as many other Members elected for three-year terms by the General Assembly as may be necessary to ensure that the total number of members of the Trusteeship Council is equally divided between those Members of the United Nations which administer trust territories and those which do not.

2. Each member of the Trusteeship Council shall designate one specially qualified person to represent it therein.

Functions and Powers

Article 87

The General Assembly and, under its authority, the Trusteeship Council, in carrying out their functions, may:

    a. consider reports submitted by the administering authority;

    b. accept petitions and examine them in consultation with the administering authority;

    c. provide for periodic visits to the respective trust territories at times agreed upon with the administering authority; and

    d. take these and other actions in conformity with the terms of the trusteeship agreements.

Article 88

The Trusteeship Council shall formulate a questionnaire on the political, economic, social, and educational advancement of the inhabitants of each trust territory, and the administering authority for each trust territory within the competence of the General Assembly shall make an annual report to the General Assembly upon the basis of such questionnaire.

Voting

Article 89

1. Each member of the Trusteeship Council shall have one vote.
2. Decisions of the Trusteeship Council shall be made by a majority of the members present and voting.

Procedure

Article 90

1. The Trusteeship Council shall adopt its own rules of procedure, including the method of selecting its President.
2. The Trusteeship Council shall meet as required in accordance with its rules, which shall include provision for the convening of meetings on the request of a majority of its members.

Article 91

The Trusteeship Council shall, when appropriate, avail itself of the assistance of the Economic and Social Council and of the specialized agencies in regard to matters with which they are respectively concerned.

CHAPTER XIV

THE INTERNATIONAL COURT OF JUSTICE

Article 92

The International Court of Justice shall be the principal judicial organ of the United Nations. It shall function in accordance with the annexed Statute, which is based upon the Statute of the Permanent Court of International Justice and forms an integral part of the present Charter.

Article 93

1. All Members of the United Nations are *ipso facto* parties to the Statute of the International Court of Justice.
2. A state which is not a Member of the United Nations may become a party to the Statute of the International Court of Justice on con-

ditions to be determined in each case by the General Assembly upon the recommendation of the Security Council.

Article 94

1. Each Member of the United Nations undertakes to comply with the decision of the International Court of Justice in any case to which it is a party.

2. If any party to a case fails to perform the obligations incumbent upon it under a judgment rendered by the Court, the other party may have recourse to the Security Council, which may, if it deems necessary, make recommendations or decide upon measures to be taken to give effect to the judgment.

Article 95

Nothing in the present Charter shall prevent Members of the United Nations from entrusting the solution of their differences to other tribunals by virtue of agreements already in existence or which may be concluded in the future.

Article 96

1. The General Assembly or the Security Council may request the International Court of Justice to give an advisory opinion on any legal question.

2. Other organs of the United Nations and specialized agencies, which may at any time be so authorized by the General Assembly, may also request advisory opinions of the Court on legal questions arising within the scope of their activities.

CHAPTER XV

THE SECRETARIAT

Article 97

The Secretariat shall comprise a Secretary-General and such staff as the Organization may require. The Secretary-General shall be appointed by the General Assembly upon the recommendation of the Security Council. He shall be the chief administrative officer of the Organization.

Article 98

The Secretary-General shall act in that capacity in all meetings of the General Assembly, of the Security Council, of the Economic and Social Council, and of the Trusteeship Council, and shall perform such other functions as are entrusted to him by these organs. The Secretary-General shall make an annual report to the General Assembly on the work of the Organization.

Article 99

The Secretary-General may bring to the attention of the Security Council any matter which in his opinion may threaten the maintenance of international peace and security.

Article 100

1. In the performance of their duties the Secretary-General and the staff shall not seek or receive instructions from any government or from any other authority external to the Organization. They shall refrain from any action which might reflect on their position as international officials responsible only to the Organization.

2. Each Member of the United Nations undertakes to respect the exclusively international character of the responsibilities of the Secretary-General and the staff and not to seek to influence them in the discharge of their responsibilities.

Article 101

1. The staff shall be appointed by the Secretary-General under regulations established by the General Assembly.

2. Appropriate staff shall be permanently assigned to the Economic and Social Council, the Trusteeship Council, and, as required, to other organs of the United Nations. These staffs shall form a part of the Secretariat.

3. The paramount consideration in the employment of the staff and in the determination of the conditions of service shall be the necessity of securing the highest standards of efficiency, competence, and integrity. Due regard shall be paid to the importance of recruiting the staff on as wide a geographical basis as possible.

CHAPTER XVI

MISCELLANEOUS PROVISIONS

Article 102

1. Every treaty and every international agreement entered into by any Member of the United Nations after the present Charter comes into force shall as soon as possible be registered with the Secretariat and published by it.

2. No party to any such treaty or international agreement which has not been registered in accordance with the provisions of paragraph 1 of this Article may invoke that treaty or agreement before any organ of the United Nations.

Article 103

In the vent of a conflict between the obligations of the Members of the United Nations under the present Charter and their obligations under any other international agreement, their obligations under the present Charter shall prevail.

Article 104

The Organization shall enjoy in the territory of each of its Members such legal capacity as may be necessary for the exercise of its functions and the fulfilment of its purposes.

Article 105

1. The Organization shall enjoy in the territory of each of its Members such privileges and immunities as are necessary for the fulfilment of its purposes.

2. Representatives of the Members of the United Nations and officials of the Organization shall similarly enjoy such privileges and immunities as are necessary for the independent exercise of their functions in connexion with the Organization.

3. The General Assembly may make recommendations with a view to determining the details of the application of paragraphs 1 and 2 of this Article or may propose conventions to the Members of the United Nations for this purpose.

CHAPTER XVII

TRANSITIONAL SECURITY ARRANGEMENTS

Article 106

Pending the coming into force of such special agreements referred to in Article 43 as in the opinion of the Security Council enable it to begin the exercise of its responsibilities under Article 42, the parties to the Four Nation Declaration, signed at Moscow, 30 October 1943, and France, shall, in accordance with the provisions of paragraph 5 of that Declaration, consult with one another and as occasion requires with other Members of the United Nations with a view to such joint action on behalf of the Organization as may be necessary for the purpose of maintaining international peace and security.

Article 107

Nothing in the present Charter shall invalidate or preclude action, in relation to any state which during the Second World War has been an enemy of any signatory to the present Charter, taken or authorized as a result of that war by the Governments having responsibility for such action.

CHAPTER XVIII

AMENDMENTS

Article 108

Amendments to the present Charter shall come into force for all Members of the United Nations when they have been adopted by a vote of two thirds of the members of the General Assembly and ratified in accordance with their respective constitutional processes by two thirds of the Members of the United Nations, including all the permanent members of the Security Council.

Article 109

1. A General Conference of the Members of the United Nations for the purpose of reviewing the present charter may be held at a date and place to be fixed by a two-thirds vote of the members of the General Assembly and by a vote of any nine members of the Security Council. Each Member of the United Nations shall have one vote in the conference.

2. Any alteration of the present Charter recommended by a two-thirds vote of the conference shall take effect when ratified in accordance with their respective constitutional processes by two thirds of the Members of the United Nations including all the permanent members of the Security Council.

3. If such a conference has not been held before the tenth annual session of the General Assembly following the coming into force of the present Charter, the proposal to call such a conference shall be placed on the agenda of that session of the General Assembly, and the conference shall be held if so decided by a majority vote of the members of the General Assembly and by a vote of any seven members of the Security Council.

CHAPTER XIX

RATIFICATION AND SIGNATURE

Article 110

1. The present Charter shall be ratified by the signatory states in accordance with their respective constitutional processes.

2. The ratifications shall be deposited with the Government of the United States of America, which shall notify all the signatory states of each deposit as well as the Secretary-General of the Organization when he has been appointed.

3. The present Charter shall come into force upon the deposit of ratifications by the Republic of China, France, the Union of Soviet Socialist Republics, the United Kingdom of Great Britain and Northern

Ireland, and the United States of America, and by a majority of the other signatory states. A protocol of the ratifications deposited shall thereupon be drawn up by the Government of the United States of America which shall communicate copies thereof to all the signatory states.

4. The states signatory to the present Charter which ratify it after it has come into force will become original Members of the United Nations on the date of the deposit of their respective ratifications.

Article 111

The present Charter, of which the Chinese, French, Russian, English, and Spanish texts are equally authentic, shall remain deposited in the archives of the Government of the United States of America. Duly certified copies thereof shall be transmitted by that Government to the Governments of the other signatory states.

In faith whereof the representatives of the Governments of the United Nations have signed the present Charter.

Done at the city of San Francisco the twenty-sixth day of June, one thousand nine hundred and forty-five.

STATUTE OF THE INTERNATIONAL COURT OF JUSTICE

Article 1

The International Court of Justice established by the Charter of the United Nations as the principal judicial organ of the United Nations shall be constituted and shall function in accordance with the provisions of the present Statute.

CHAPTER I

ORGANIZATION OF THE COURT

Article 2

The Court shall be composed of a body of independent judges, elected regardless of their nationality from among persons of high moral character, who possess the qualifications required in their respective countries for appointment to the highest judicial offices, or are jurisconsults of recognized competence in international law.

Article 3

1. The Court shall consist of fifteen members, no two of whom may be nationals of the same state.

2. A person who for the purposes of membership in the Court could be regarded as a national of more than one state shall be

deemed to be a national of the one in which he ordinarily exercises civil and political rights.

Article 4

1. The members of the Court shall be elected by the General Assembly and by the Security Council from a list of persons nominated by the national groups in the Permanent Court of Arbitration, in accordance with the following provisions.

2. In the case of Members of the United Nations not represented in the Permanent Court of Arbitration, candidates shall be nominated by national groups appointed for this purpose by their governments under the same conditions as those prescribed for members of the Permanent Court of Arbitration by Article 44 of the Convention of The Hague of 1907 for the pacific settlement of international disputes.

3. The conditions under which a state which is a party to the present Statute but is not a Member of the United Nations may participate in electing the members of the Court shall, in the absence of a special agreement, be laid down by the General Assembly upon recommendation of the Security Council.

Article 5

1. At least three months before the date of the election, the Secretary-General of the United Nations shall address a written request to the members of the Permanent Court of Arbitration belonging to the states which are parties to the present Statute, and to the members of the national groups appointed under Article 4, paragraph 2, inviting them to undertake, within a given time, by national groups, the nomination of persons in a position to accept the duties of a member of the Court.

2. No group may nominate more than four persons, not more than two of whom shall be of their own nationality. In no case may the number of candidates nominated by a group be more than double the number of seats to be filled.

Article 6

Before making these nominations, each national group is recommended to consult its highest court of justice, its legal faculties and schools of law, and its national academies and national sections of international academies devoted to the study of law.

Article 7

1. The Secretary-General shall prepare a list in alphabetical order of all the persons thus nominated. Save as provided in Article 12, paragraph 2, these shall be the only persons eligible.

2. The Secretary-General shall submit this list to the General Assembly and to the Security Council.

Article 8

The General Assembly and the Security Council shall proceed independently of one another to elect the members of the Court.

Article 9

At every election, the electors shall bear in mind not only that the persons to be elected should individually possess the qualifications required, but also that in the body as a whole the representation of the main forms of civilization and of the principal legal systems of the world should be assured.

Article 10

1. Those candidates who obtain an absolute majority of votes in the General Assembly and in the Security Council shall be considered as elected.

2. Any vote of the Security Council, whether for the election of judges or for the appointment of members of the conference envisaged in Article 12, shall be taken without any distinction between permanent and non-permanent members of the Security Council.

3. In the event of more than one national of the same state obtaining an absolute majority of the votes both of the General Assembly and of the Security Council, the eldest of these only shall be considered as elected.

Article 11

If, after the first meeting held for the purpose of the election, one or more seats remain to be filled, a second and, if necessary, a third meeting shall take place.

Article 12

1. If, after the third meeting, one or more seats still remain unfilled, a joint conference consisting of six members, three appointed by the General Assembly and three by the Security Council, may be formed at any time at the request of either the General Assembly or the Security Council, for the purpose of choosing by the vote of an absolute majority one name for each seat still vacant, to submit to the General Assembly and the Security Council for their respective acceptance.

2. If the joint conference is unanimously agreed upon any person who fulfils the required conditions, he may be included in its list, even though he was not included in the list of nominations referred to in Article 7.

3. If the joint conference is satisfied that it will not be successful in procuring an election, those members of the Court who have already been elected shall, within a period to be fixed by the Security Council, proceed to fill the vacant seats by selection from among

those candidates who have obtained votes either in the General Assembly or in the Security Council.

4. In the event of an equality of vote among the judges, the eldest judge shall have a casting vote.

Article 13

1. The members of the Court shall be elected for nine years and may be re-elected; provided, however, that of the judges elected at the first election, the terms of five judges shall expire at the end of three years and the terms of five more judges shall expire at the end of six years.

2. The judges whose terms are to expire at the end of the above-mentioned initial periods of three and six years shall be chosen by lot to be drawn by the Secretary-General immediately after the first election has been completed.

3. The members of the Court shall continue to discharge their duties until their places have been filled. Though replaced, they shall finish any cases which they may have begun.

4. In the case of the resignation of a member of the Court, the resignation shall be addressed to the President of the Court for transmission to the Secretary-General. This last notification makes the place vacant.

Article 14

Vacancies shall be filled by the same method as that laid down for the first election, subject to the following provision: the Secretary-General shall, within one month of the occurrence of the vacancy, proceed to issue the invitations provided for in Article 5, and the date of the election shall be fixed by the Security Council.

Article 15

A member of the Court elected to replace a member whose term of office has not expired shall hold office for the remainder of his predecessor's term.

Article 16

1. No member of the Court may exercise any political or administrative function, or engage in any other occupation of a professional nature.

2. Any doubt on this point shall be settled by the decision of the Court.

Article 17

1. No member of the Court may act as agent, counsel, or advocate in any case.

2. No member may participate in the decision of any case in which he has previously taken part as agent, counsel, or advocate for one

of the parties, or as a member of a national or international court, or of a commission of enquiry, or in any other capacity.

3. Any doubt on this point shall be settled by the decision of the Court.

Article 18

1. No member of the Court can be dismissed unless, in the unanimous opinion of the other members he has ceased to fulfil the required conditions.

2. Formal notification thereof shall be made to the Secretary-General by the Registrar.

3. This notification makes the place vacant.

Article 19

The members of the Court, when engaged on the business of the Court, shall enjoy diplomatic privileges and immunities.

Article 20

Every member of the Court shall, before taking up his duties, make a solemn declaration in open court that he will exercise his powers impartially and conscientiously.

Article 21

1. The Court shall elect its President and Vice-President for three years; they may be re-elected.

2. The Court shall appoint its Registrar and may provide for the appointment of such other officers as may be necessary.

Article 22

1. The seat of the Court shall be established at The Hague. This, however, shall not prevent the Court from sitting and exercising its functions elsewhere whenever the Court considers it desirable.

2. The President and the Registrar shall reside at the seat of the Court.

Article 23

1. The Court shall remain permanently in session, except during the judicial vacations, the dates and duration of which shall be fixed by the Court.

2. Members of the Court are entitled to periodic leave, the dates and duration of which shall be fixed by the Court, having in mind the distance between The Hague and the home of each judge.

3. Members of the Court shall be bound, unless they are on leave or prevented from attending by illness or other serious reasons duly explained to the President, to hold themselves permanently at the disposal of the Court.

Article 24

1. If, for some special reason, a member of the Court considers that he should not take part in the decision of a particular case, he shall so inform the President.

2. If the President considers that for some special reason one of the members of the Court should not sit in a particular case, he shall give him notice accordingly.

3. If in any such case the member of the Court and the President disagree, the matter shall be settled by the decision of the Court.

Article 25

1. The full Court shall sit except when it is expressly provided otherwise in the present Statute.

2. Subject to the condition that the number of judges available to constitute the Court is not thereby reduced below eleven, the Rules of the Court may provide for allowing one or more judges, according to circumstances and in rotation, to be dispensed from sitting.

3. A quorum of nine judges shall suffice to constitute the Court.

Article 26

1. The Court may from time to time form one or more chambers, composed of three or more judges as the Court may determine, for dealing with particular categories of cases; for example, labour cases and cases relating to transit and communications.

2. The Court may at any time form a chamber for dealing with a particular case. The number of judges to constitute such a chamber shall be determined by the Court with the approval of the parties.

3. Cases shall be heard and determined by the chambers provided for in this article if the parties so request.

Article 27

A judgment given by any of the chambers provided for in Articles 26 and 29 shall be considered as rendered by the Court.

Article 28

The chambers provided for in Articles 26 and 29 may, with the consent of the parties, sit and exercise their functions elsewhere than at The Hague.

Article 29

With a view to the speedy dispatch of business, the Court shall form annually a chamber composed of five judges which, at the request of the parties, may hear and determine cases by summary procedure. In addition, two judges shall be selected for the purpose of replacing judges who find it impossible to sit.

Article 30

1. The Court shall frame rules for carrying out its functions. In particular, it shall lay down rules of procedure.

2. The Rules of the Court may provide for assessors to sit with the Court or with any of its chambers, without the right to vote.

Article 31

1. Judges of the nationality of each of the parties shall retain their right to sit in the case before the Court.

2. If the Court includes upon the Bench a judge of the nationality of one of the parties, any other party may choose a person to sit as judge. Such person shall be chosen preferably from among those persons who have been nominated as candidates as provided in Articles 4 and 5.

3. If the Court includes upon the Bench no judge of the nationality of the parties, each of these parties may proceed to choose a judge as provided in paragraph 2 of this Article.

4. The provisions of this Article shall apply to the case of Articles 26 and 29. In such cases, the President shall request one or, if necessary, two of the members of the Court forming the chamber to give place to the members of the Court of the nationality of the parties concerned, and, failing such, or if they are unable to be present, to the judges specially chosen by the parties.

5. Should there be several parties in the same interest, they shall, for the purpose of the preceding provisions, be reckoned as one party only. Any doubt upon this point shall be settled by the decision of the Court.

6. Judges chosen as laid down in paragraphs 2, 3, and 4 of this Article shall fulfil the conditions required by Articles 2, 17 (paragraph 2), 20, and 24 of the present Statute. They shall take part in the decision on terms of complete equality with their colleagues.

Article 32

1. Each member of the Court shall receive an annual salary.

2. The President shall receive a special annual allowance.

3. The Vice-President shall receive a special allowance for every day on which he acts as President.

4. The judges chosen under Article 31, other than members of the Court, shall receive compensation for each day on which they exercise their functions.

5. These salaries, allowances, and compensation shall be fixed by the General Assembly. They may not be decreased during the term of office.

6. The salary of the Registrar shall be fixed by the General Assembly on the proposal of the Court.

7. Regulations made by the General Assembly shall fix the

conditions under which retirement pensions may be given to members of the Court and to the Registrar, and the conditions under which members of the Court and the Registrar shall have their travelling expenses refunded.

8. The above salaries, allowances, and compensation shall be free of all taxation.

Article 33

The expenses of the Court shall be borne by the United Nations in such a manner as shall be decided by the General Assembly.

CHAPTER II
COMPETENCE OF THE COURT

Article 34

1. Only states may be parties in cases before the Court.

2. The Court, subject to and in conformity with its Rules, may request of public international organizations information relevant to cases before it, and shall receive such information presented by such organizations on their own initiative.

3. Whenever the construction of the constituent instrument of a public international organization or of an international convention adopted thereunder is in question in a case before the Court, the Registrar shall so notify the public international organization concerned and shall communicate to it copies of all the written proceedings.

Article 35

1. The Court shall be open to the states parties to the present Statute.

2. The conditions under which the Court shall be open to other states shall, subject to the special provisions contained in treaties in force, be laid down by the Security Council, but in no case shall such conditions place the parties in a position of inequality before the Court.

3. When a state which is not a Member of the United Nations is a party to a case, the Court shall fix the amount which that party is to contribute towards the expenses of the Court. This provision shall not apply if such state is bearing a share of the expenses of the Court.

Article 36

1. The jurisdiction of the Court comprises all cases which the parties refer to it and all matters specially provided for in the Charter of the United Nations or in treaties and conventions in force.

2. The states parties to the present Statute may at any time de-

clare that they recognize as compulsory *ipso facto* and without special agreement, in relation to any other state accepting the same obligation, the jurisdiction of the Court in all legal disputes concerning:

    a. the interpretation of a treaty;
    b. any question of international law;
    c. the existence of any fact which, if established, would constitute a breach of an international obligation;
    d. the nature or extent of the reparation to be made for the breach of an international obligation.

3. The declarations referred to above may be made unconditionally or on condition of reciprocity on the part of several or certain states, or for a certain time.

4. Such declarations shall be deposited with the Secretary-General of the United Nations, who shall transmit copies thereof to the parties to the Statute and to the Registrar of the Court.

5. Declarations made under Article 36 of the Statute of the Permanent Court of International Justice and which are still in force shall be deemed, as between the parties to the present Statute, to be acceptances of the compulsory jurisdiction of the International Court of Justice for the period which they still have to run and in accordance with their terms.

6. In the event of a dispute as to whether the Court has jurisdiction, the matter shall be settled by the decision of the Court.

Article 37

Whenever a treaty or convention in force provides for reference of a matter to a tribunal to have been instituted by the League of Nations, or to the Permanent Court of International Justice, the matter shall, as between the parties to the present Statute, be referred to the International Court of Justice.

Article 38

1. The Court, whose function is to decide in accordance with international law such disputes as are submitted to it, shall apply:

    a. international conventions, whether general or particular, establishing rules expressly recognized by the contesting states;
    b. international custom, as evidence of a general practice accepted as law;
    c. the general principles of law recognized by civilized nations;
    d. subject to the provisions of Article 59, judicial decisions and the teachings of the most highly qualified publicists of the various nations, as subsidiary means for the determination of rules of law.

2. This provision shall not prejudice the power of the Court to decide a case *ex aequo et bono*, if the parties agree thereto.

CHAPTER III

PROCEDURE

Article 39

1. The official languages of the Court shall be French and English. If the parties agree that the case shall be conducted in French, the judgment shall be delivered in French. If the parties agree that the case shall be conducted in English, the judgment shall be delivered in English.

2. In the absence of an agreement as to which language shall be employed, each party may, in the pleadings, use the language which it prefers; the decision of the Court shall be given in French and English. In this case the Court shall at the same time determine which of the two texts shall be considered as authoritative.

3. The Court shall, at the request of any party, authorize a language other than French or English to be used by that party.

Article 40

1. Cases are brought before the Court, as the case may be, either by the notification of the special agreement or by a written application addressed to the Registrar. In either case the subject of the dispute and the parties shall be indicated.

2. The Registrar shall forthwith communicate the application to all concerned.

3. He shall also notify the Members of the United Nations through the Secretary-General, and also any other states entitled to appear before the Court.

Article 41

1. The Court shall have the power to indicate, if it considers that circumstances so require, any provisional measures which ought to be taken to preserve the respective rights of either party.

2. Pending the final decision, notice of the measures suggested shall forthwith be given to the parties and to the Security Council.

Article 42

1. The parties shall be represented by agents.

2. They may have the assistance of counsel or advocates before the Court.

3. The agents, counsel, and advocates of parties before the Court shall enjoy the privileges and immunities necessary to the independent exercise of their duties.

Article 43

1. The procedure shall consist of two parts: written and oral.

2. The written proceedings shall consist of the communication to

the Court and to the parties of memorials, counter-memorials and, if necessary, replies; also all papers and documents in support.

3. These communications shall be made through the Registrar, in the order and within the time fixed by the Court.

4. A certified copy of every document produced by one party shall be communicated to the other party.

5. The oral proceedings shall consist of the hearing by the Court of witnesses, experts, agents, counsel, and advocates.

Article 44

1. For the service of all notices upon persons other than the agents, counsel, and advocates, the Court shall apply direct to the government of the state upon whose territory the notice has to be served.

2. The same provision shall apply whenever steps are to be taken to procure evidence on the spot.

Article 45

The hearing shall be under the control of the President or, if he is unable to preside, of the Vice-President; if neither is able to preside, the senior judge present shall preside.

Article 46

The hearing in Court shall be public, unless the Court shall decide otherwise, or unless the parties demand that the public be not admitted.

Article 47

1. Minutes shall be made at each hearing and signed by the Registrar and the President.

2. These minutes alone shall be authentic.

Article 48

The Court shall make orders for the conduct of the case, shall decide the form and time in which each party must conclude its arguments, and make all arrangements connected with the taking of evidence.

Article 49

The Court may, even before the hearing begins, call upon the agents to produce any document or to supply any explanations. Formal note shall be taken of any refusal.

Article 50

The Court may, at any time, entrust any individual, body, bureau, commission, or other organization that it may select, with the task of carrying out an enquiry or giving an expert opinion.

Article 51

During the hearing any relevant questions are to be put to the witnesses and experts under the conditions laid down by the Court in the rules of procedure referred to in Article 30.

Article 52

After the Court has received the proofs and evidence within the time specified for the purpose, it may refuse to accept any further oral or written evidence that one party may desire to present unless the other side consents.

Article 53

1. Whenever one of the parties does not appear before the Court, or fails to defend its case, the other party may call upon the Court to decide in favour of its claim.

2. The Court must, before doing so, satisfy itself, not only that it has jurisdiction in accordance with Articles 36 and 37, but also that the claim is well founded in fact and law.

Article 54

1. When, subject to the control of the Court, the agents, counsel, and advocates have completed their presentation of the case, the President shall declare the hearing closed.

2. The Court shall withdraw to consider the judgment.

3. The deliberations of the Court shall take place in private and remain secret.

Article 55

1. All questions shall be decided by a majority of the judges present.

2. In the event of an equality of votes, the President or the judge who acts in his place shall have a casting vote.

Article 56

1. The judgment shall state the reasons on which it is based.

2. It shall contain the names of the judges who have taken part in the decision.

Article 57

If the judgment does not represent in whole or in part the unanimous opinion of the judges, any judge shall be entitled to deliver a separate opinion.

Article 58

The judgment shall be signed by the President and by the Registrar. It shall be read in open court, due notice having been given to the agents.

Article 59

The decision of the Court has no binding force except between the parties and in respect of that particular case.

Article 60

The judgment is final and without appeal. In the event of dispute as to the meaning or scope of the judgment, the Court shall construe it upon the request of any party.

Article 61

1. An application for revision of a judgment may be made only when it is based upon the discovery of some fact of such a nature as to be a decisive factor, which fact was, when the judgment was given, unknown to the Court and also to the party claiming revision, always provided that such ignorance was not due to negligence.

2. The proceedings for revision shall be opened by a judgment of the Court expressly recording the existence of the new fact, recognizing that it has such a character as to lay the case open to revision, and declaring the application admissible on this ground.

3. The Court may require previous compliance with the terms of the judgment before it admits proceedings in revision.

4. The application for revision must be made at latest within six months of the discovery of the new fact.

5. No application for revision may be made after the lapse of ten years from the date of the judgment.

Article 62

1. Should a state consider that it has an interest of a legal nature which may be affected by the decision in the case, it may submit a request to the Court to be permitted to intervene.

2. It shall be for the Court to decide upon this request.

Article 63

1. Whenever the construction of a convention to which states other than those concerned in the case are parties is in question, the Registrar shall notify all such states forthwith.

2. Every state so notified has the right to intervene in the proceedings; but if it uses this right, the construction given by the judgment will be equally binding upon it.

Article 64

Unless otherwise decided by the Court, each party shall bear its own costs.

CHAPTER IV

ADVISORY OPINIONS

Article 65

1. The Court may give an advisory opinion on any legal question at the request of whatever body may be authorized by or in accordance with the Charter of the United Nations to make such a request.
2. Questions upon which the advisory opinion of the Court is asked shall be laid before the Court by means of a written request containing an exact statement of the question upon which an opinion is required, and accompanied by all documents likely to throw light upon the question.

Article 66

1. The Registrar shall forthwith give notice of the request for an advisory opinion to all states entitled to appear before the Court.
2. The Registrar shall also, by means of a special and direct communication, notify any state entitled to appear before the Court or international organization considered by the Court, or, should it not be sitting, by the President, as likely to be able to furnish information on the question, that the Court will be prepared to receive, within a time limit to be fixed by the President, written statements, or to hear, at a public sitting to be held for the purpose, oral statements relating to the question.
3. Should any such state entitled to appear before the Court have failed to receive the special communication referred to in paragraph 2 of this Article, such state may express a desire to submit a written statement or to be heard; and the Court will decide.
4. States and organizations having presented written or oral statements or both shall be permitted to comment on the statements made by other states or organizations in the form, to the extent, and within the time limits which the Court, or, should it not be sitting, the President, shall decide in each particular case. Accordingly, the Registrar shall in due time communicate any such written statements to states and organizations having submitted similar statements.

Article 67

The Court shall deliver its advisory opinions in open court, notice having been given to the Secretary-General and to the representatives of Members of the United Nations, of other states and of international organizations immediately concerned.

Article 68

In the exercise of its advisory functions the Court shall further be guided by the provisions of the present Statute which apply in contentious cases to the extent to which it recognizes them to be applicable.

CHAPTER V

AMENDMENT

Article 69

Amendments to the present Statute shall be effected by the same procedure as is provided by the Charter of the United Nations for amendments to that Charter, subject however to any provisions which the General Assembly upon recommendation of the Security Council may adopt concerning the participation of states which are parties to the present Statute but are not Members of the United Nations.

Article 70

The Court shall have power to propose such amendments to the present Statute as it may deem necessary, through written communications to the Secretary-General, for consideration in conformity with the provisions of Article 69.

Appendix 2
United Nations
Membership
(1 January 1994)

Member states	Date of admission	Estimated population	Percentage of UN budget	No. of staff subject to geographic distribution
Afghanistan	19 November 1946	16 433 000	0.01	9
Albania	14 December 1955	3 250 000	0.01	1
Algeria	8 October 1962	25 324 000	0.16	18
Andorra	28 July 1993	52 000	*	*
Angola	1 December 1976	10 020 000	0.01	1
Antigua and Barbuda	11 November 1981	77 000	0.01	4
Argentina	24 October 1945	32 609 000	0.57	26
Armenia	2 March 1992	3 376 000	0.13	0
Australia	1 November 1945	17 086 000	1.51	31
Austria	14 December 1955	7 823 000	0.75	21
Azerbaijan	2 March 1992	7 137 000	0.22	0
Bahamas	18 September 1973	253 000	0.02	1
Bahrain	21 September 1971	503 000	0.03	0
Bangladesh	17 September 1974	104 766 143	0.01	13
Barbados	9 December 1966	257 082	0.01	8
Belarus	2 March 1992	10 297 000	0.48	13
Belgium	27 December 1945	9 845 000	1.06	24
Belize	25 September 1981	194 000	0.01	3
Benin	20 September 1960	4 889 000	0.01	6
Bhutan	21 September 1971	1 517 000	0.01	4
Bolivia	14 November 1945	7 400 000	0.01	5
Bosnia and Herzegovina	22 May 1992	4 300 000	0.04	0
Botswana	17 October 1966	1 348 000	0.01	1
Brazil	24 October 1945	153 322 000	1.59	37
Brunei Darussalam	21 September 1984	266 000	0.03	0
Bulgaria	14 December 1955	8 977 000	0.13	8
Burkina Faso	20 September 1960	9 242 000	0.01	7

Member states	Date of admission	Estimated population	Percentage of UN budget	No. of staff subject to geographic distribution
Burundi	18 September 1962	5 620 000	0.01	11
Cambodia	14 December 1955	8 246 000	0.01	2
Cameroon	20 September 1960	11 834 000	0.01	14
Canada	9 November 1945	26 992 000	3.11	58
Cape Verde	16 September 1975	370 000	0.01	1
Central African Republic	20 September 1960	3 039 000	0.01	4
Chad	20 September 1960	5 679 000	0.01	3
Chile	24 October 1945	13 386 000	0.08	27
China	24 October 1945	1 160 017 000	0.77	43
Colombia	5 November 1945	32 987 000	0.13	10
Comoros	12 November 1975	551 000	0.01	2
Congo	20 September 1960	2 271 000	0.01	5
Costa Rica	2 November 1945	3 030 000	0.01	3
Côte d'Ivoire	20 September 1960	11 998 000	0.02	12
Croatia	22 May 1992	4 700 000	0.13	2
Cuba	24 October 1945	10 695 000	0.09	10
Cyprus	20 September 1960	707 000	0.02	5
Czech Republic	19 January 1993	10 400 000	0.42	5
Democratic People's Republic of Korea	17 September 1991	21 773 000	0.05	0
Denmark	24 October 1945	5 140 000	0.65	13
Djibouti	20 September 1977	409 000	0.01	1
Dominica	18 December 1978	83 000	0.01	1
Dominican Republic	24 October 1945	7 170 000	0.02	7
Ecuador	21 December 1945	9 623 000	0.03	4
Egypt	24 October 1945	54 609 000	0.07	14
El Salvador	24 October 1945	5 252 000	0.01	4
Equatorial Guinea	12 November 1968	356 000	0.01	3
Eritrea	28 May 1993	*	0.01	0
Estonia	17 September 1991	1 565 000	0.07	0
Ethiopia	13 November 1945	53 383 000	0.01	26
Fiji	13 October 1970	736 000	0.01	5
Finland	14 December 1955	4 986 000	0.57	10
Former Yugoslav Republic of Macedonia	8 April 1993	1 900 000	0.02	0
France	24 October 1945	56 720 000	6.00	113
Gabon	20 September 1960	1 172 000	0.02	2
Gambia	21 September 1965	861 000	0.01	7
Georgia	31 July 1992	5 400 000	0.21	0
Germany	18 September 1973	79 973 000	8.93	128

continued on page 158

Member states	Date of admission	Estimated population	Percentage of UN budget	No. of staff subject to geographic distribution
Ghana	8 March 1957	15 028 000	0.01	15
Greece	25 October 1945	10 269 000	0.35	13
Grenada	17 September 1974	85 000	0.01	3
Guatemala	21 November 1945	9 197 000	0.02	7
Guinea	12 December 1958	5 756 000	0.01	6
Guinea-Bissau	17 September 1974	965 000	0.01	1
Guyana	20 September 1966	796 000	0.01	16
Haiti	24 October 1945	6 625 000	0.01	6
Honduras	17 December 1945	5 105 000	0.01	3
Hungary	14 December 1955	10 341 000	0.18	7
Iceland	19 November 1946	258 000	0.03	7
India	30 October 1945	843 931 000	0.36	42
Indonesia	28 September 1950	179 322 000	0.16	6
Iran (Islamic Republic of)	24 October 1945	58 798 000	0.77	19
Iraq	21 December 1945	18 920 000	0.13	12
Ireland	14 December 1955	3 523 000	0.18	15
Israel	11 May 1949	5 037 000	0.23	15
Italy	14 December 1955	57 690 000	4.29	65
Jamaica	18 September 1962	2 420 000	0.01	18
Japan	18 December 1956	123 921 000	12.45	86
Jordan	14 December 1955	4 010 000	0.01	15
Kazakhstan	2 March 1992	16 793 000	0.35	0
Kenya	16 December 1963	25 905 000	0.01	12
Kuwait	14 May 1963	2 143 000	0.25	0
Kyrgystan	2 March 1992	4 422 000	0.06	0
Lao People's Democratic Republic	14 December 1955	4 139 000	0.01	1
Latvia	17 September 1991	2 686 000	0.13	0
Lebanon	24 October 1945	2 701 000	0.01	20
Lesotho	17 October 1966	1 774 000	0.01	7
Liberia	2 November 1945	2 705 000	0.01	8
Libyan Arab Jamahiriya	14 December 1955	4 083 000	0.24	6
Liechtenstein	18 September 1990	29 000	0.01	0
Lithuania	17 September 1991	3 739 000	0.15	0
Luxembourg	24 October 1945	385 000	0.06	4
Madagascar	20 September 1960	11 197 000	0.01	9
Malawi	1 December 1964	8 556 000	0.01	10
Malaysia	17 September 1957	17 756 000	0.12	15
Maldives	21 September 1965	223 000	0.01	0
Mali	28 September 1960	8 156 000	0.01	10
Malta	1 December 1964	356 000	0.01	6
Marshall Islands	17 September 1991	48 000	0.01	0

Member states	Date of admission	Estimated population	Percentage of UN budget	No. of staff subject to geographic distribution
Mauritania	27 October 1961	2 036 000	0.01	6
Mauritius	24 April 1968	1 070 000	0.01	11
Mexico	7 November 1945	87 836 000	0.88	24
Micronesia (Federated State of)	17 September 1991	99 000	0.01	0
Monaco	28 May 1993	28 000	0.01	0
Mongolia	27 October 1961	2 190 000	0.01	1
Morocco	12 November 1956	25 061 000	0.03	11
Mozambique	16 September 1975	15 656 000	0.01	1
Myanmar	19 April 1948	41 675 000	0.01	6
Namibia	23 April 1990	1 781 000	0.01	0
Nepal	14 December 1955	18 916 000	0.01	8
Netherlands	10 December 1945	15 131 000	1.50	36
New Zealand	24 October 1945	3 380 000	0.24	12
Nicaragua	24 October 1945	3 999 000	0.01	7
Niger	20 September 1960	7 732 000	0.01	4
Nigeria	7 October 1960	108 542 000	0.20	16
Norway	27 November 1945	4 262 000	0.55	13
Oman	7 October 1971	1 502 000	0.03	2
Pakistan	30 September 1947	115 520 000	0.06	13
Panama	13 November 1945	2 466 000	0.02	3
Papua New Guinea	10 October 1975	3 699 000	0.01	2
Paraguay	24 October 1945	4 277 000	0.02	1
Peru	31 October 1945	21 998 000	0.06	17
Philippines	24 October 1945	61 480 000	0.07	71
Poland	24 October 1945	38 244 000	0.47	13
Portugal	14 December 1955	9 868 000	0.20	5
Qatar	21 September 1971	486 000	0.05	1
Republic of Korea	17 September 1991	43 500 000	0.69	1
Republic of Moldova	2 March 1992	4 373 000	0.15	0
Romania	14 December 1955	23 201 000	0.17	5
Russian Federation	24 October 1945	148 485 000	6.71	145
Rwanda	18 September 1962	7 165 000	0.01	4
Saint Kitts and Nevis	23 September 1983	44 000	0.01	2
Saint Lucia	18 September 1979	151 000	0.01	4
Saint Vincent and the Grenadines	16 September 1980	116 000	0.01	3
Samoa	15 December 1976	164 000	0.01	2
San Marino	2 March 1992	24 000	0.01	0

continued on page 160

Member states	Date of admission	Estimated population	Percentage of UN budget	No. of staff subject to geographic distribution
São Tome and Pri̇́ncipe	16 September 1975	121 000	0.01	0
Saudi Arabia	24 October 1945	14 870 000	0.96	4
Senegal	28 September 1960	7 327 000	0.01	15
Seychelles	21 September 1976	68 000	0.01	2
Sierra Leone	27 September 1961	4 151 000	0.01	15
Singapore	21 September 1965	3 003 000	0.12	11
Slovak Republic	19 January 1993	5 300 000	0.13	2
Slovenia	22 May 1992	1 800 000	0.09	1
Solomon Islands	19 September 1978	321 000	0.01	0
Somalia	20 September 1960	7 497 000	0.01	9
South Africa	7 November 1945	35 282 000	0.41	11
Spain	14 December 1955	39 025 000	1.98	28
Sri Lanka	14 December 1955	16 993 000	0.01	9
Sudan	12 November 1956	25 204 000	0.01	8
Surinam	4 December 1975	422 000	0.01	3
Swaziland	24 September 1968	768 000	0.01	4
Sweden	19 November 1946	8 642 000	1.11	24
Syrian Arab Republic	24 October 1945	12 116 000	0.04	9
Tajikistan	2 March 1992	5 357 000	0.05	0
Thailand	16 December 1946	57 196 000	0.11	28
Togo	20 September 1960	3 531 000	0.01	5
Trinidad and Tobago	18 September 1962	1 253 000	0.05	18
Tunisia	12 November 1956	8 180 000	0.03	17
Turkey	24 October 1945	57 326 000	0.27	11
Turkmenistan	2 March 1992	3 714 000	0.06	0
Uganda	25 October 1962	16 583 000	0.01	14
Ukraine	24 October 1945	51 944 000	1.87	24
United Arab Emirates	9 December 1971	1 589 000	0.21	1
United Kingdom of Great Britain and Northern Ireland	24 October 1945	57 411 000	5.02	83
United Republic of Tanzania	14 December 1961	25 635 000	0.01	19
United States of America	24 October 1945	253 887 000	25.00	371
Uruguay	18 December 1945	3 096 000	0.04	10
Uzbekistan	2 March 1992	20 708 000	0.26	0
Vanuatu	15 September 1981	147 000	0.01	0
Venezuela	15 November 1945	18 105 000	0.49	8
Viet Nam	20 September 1977	66 200 000	0.01	3

Member states	Date of admission	Estimated population	Percentage of UN budget	No. of staff subject to geographic distribution
Yemen	30 September 1947	11 282 000	0.01	9
Yugoslavia	24 October 1945	23 991 000	0.14	11
Zaire	20 September 1960	36 672 000	0.01	15
Zambia	1 December 1964	8 023 000	0.01	9
Zimbabwe	25 August 1980	9 369 000	0.01	6

* Indicates information not available at time of going to press.

Appendix 3
States or Territories which are not UN Members

(a) *Parties to the Statute of the International Court of Justice*
Nauru
Switzerland
(b) *Territories which participate in certain UN activities*
Tonga
Tuvalu (formerly Ellice Islands)
(c) *Former colony, now independent*
Kiribati (formerly Gilbert Islands)
(d) *Territory under UN strategic trusteeship system*
Palau
(e) *Other territories within the purview of the UN committee on decolonisation*
American Samoa*
Anguilla*
Bermuda*
British Virgin Islands*
Cayman Islands*
Falkland Islands/Malvinas*
Gibraltar*
Guam*
Montserrat*
New Caledonia
Pitcairn
St Helena*
Tokelau*
Turks and Caicos Islands*
US Virgin Islands*
Western Sahara (formerly administered by Spain, now claimed by Morocco, but this was disputed by the Popular Front for the Liberation of Sakiet and Hamra y Rio de Ore – POLISARIO)
(f) *Other dependent territory*
Hong Kong (reverts to Chinese rule in 1997)

* Administering authority transmits information under Article 73(e) of the Charter.

Further Reading

Adams, Valerie, *Chemical Warfare, Chemical Disarmament* (London: Macmillan, 1989).

Baehr, Peter R. and Leon Gordenker, *The United Nations: Reality and ideal* (New York: Praeger, 1984)

Baehr, P. and Leon Gordenker, *The United Nations in the 1990s*, second edn (London: Macmillan, 1994).

Bailey, Sydney D., *The General Assembly of the United Nations*, second edn, reprinted (Westport, CT: Greenwood, 1978).

Bailey, Sydney D., *How Wars End*, 2 vols (Oxford: Clarendon Press, 1982).

Bailey, Sydney D., *Peaceful Settlement of International Disputes*, third edn (New York: UN Institute for Training and Research, 1970).

Bailey, Sydney D., *The Procedure of the UN Security Council*, second edn (Oxford: Clarendon Press, 1988).

Bailey, Sydney D., *The Secretariat of the United Nations*, second edn reprinted (Westport, CT: Greenwood, 1978).

Bailey, Sydney D., *War and Conscience in the Nuclear Age* (London: Macmillan, 1987).

Barnaby, Frank, *The Role and Control of Weapons in the 1990s* (London: Routledge, 1992).

Bellamy, Ian, *A Basis for Arms Control* (Aldershot: Dartmouth, 1991).

Berridge, G.R., *Return to the UN* (London: Macmillan, 1991).

Brownlie, Ian (ed.), *Basic Documents on Human Rights* (Oxford: Clarendon Press, third edn, 1992).

Carter, April, *Success and Failure in Arms Control Negotiations* (Oxford: Oxford University Press, 1989).

Donnelly, J., *The Concept of Human Rights* (London: Croom Helm, 1985).

Falconer, Alan D. (ed.), *Understanding Human Rights* (Dublin: Irish School of Ecumenics, 1980).

Franck, Thomas M., *Nation against Nation: What happened to the U.N. dream and what the U.S. can do about it* (Oxford: Oxford University Press, 1985).

Gates, David, *Non-offensive Defence* (London: Macmillan, 1991).

Goldblat, Jozef, *Agreements for Arms Control: A critical survey* (London: Taylor and Francis, 1982, for the Stockholm International Peace Research Institute).

Hammarskjöld, Dag, *Markings*, translated by Leif Sjoberg and W. H. Auden (London: Faber, 1964).

Hazzard, Shirley, *Defeat of an Ideal: A study of the self-destruction of the United Nations* (London: Macmillan, 1973).

Hoffman, Mark, *UK Arms Control in the 1990s* (Manchester: Manchester University Press, 1990).

Holst, Kaveli, *Peace and War* (Cambridge: Cambridge University Press, 1991).

Human Rights: A compilation of international instruments (New York: United Nations, 1993).

Humphrey, John P., *Human Rights and the United Nations: A great adventure* (New York: Transnational, 1984).

James, Alan, *Peacekeeping in International Politics* (London: Macmillan, 1990).

Jensen E. (ed.), *The United Kingdom – the United Nations* (London: Macmillan, 1990).

Lie, Trygve, *In the Cause of Peace* (New York: Macmillan, 1954).

Luard, Evan, *A History of the United Nations*, Volume 1: *The Years of Western Domination, 1945–1955* (London: Macmillan, 1982); Volume 2: *The Era of Decolonisation, 1955–1965* (London: Macmillan, 1988).

Luard, Evan, *The United Nations: How it works and what it does* (London: Macmillan, 1979).

Moynihan, Daniel Patrick, with Suzanne Weaver, *A Dangerous Place* (London: Secker & Warburg, 1979).

Nickell, James W., *Making Sense of Human Rights* (Berkeley: University of California Press, 1987).

Randle, Michael and Paul Rogers, *Alternatives in European Security* (Aldershot: Dartmouth, 1990).

Reid, Escott, *On Duty: A Canadian at the making of the United Nations* (Ohio: Kent State University Press, 1983).

Rikhye, Indar Jit, and Kjell Skelsback, *The United Nations and Peacekeeping* (London, Macmillan, 1990).

Rikhye, Indar Jit, *Military Adviser to the Secretary-General: UN peacekeeping and the Congo crisis* (London, Hurst; New York: St. Martin's, 1993).

Roberts, Adam, and Benedict Kingsbury (eds), *United Nations, Divided World*, second edn (Oxford: Clarendon Press, 1993).

Rodley, Nigel, *To Loose the Bands of Wickedness* (London: Brassey's, 1992).

Rosas, Allan, and Jan Helgesen, *Human Rights in a Changing East-West Perspective* (London: Pinter, 1990).

Rosas, Allan, and Jan Helgesen, *The Strength of Diversity* (London: Macmillan, 1992).

Russell, Ruth B., assisted by Jeanette E. Muther, *A History of the United Nations Charter* (Washington: Brookings; London: Faber, 1958).

Sieghart, Paul, *The Lawful Rights of Mankind* (Oxford: Oxford University Press, 1985).

Sims, Nicholas A., *Approaches to Disarmament*, second edn (London: Quaker Peace and Service, 1979).

Sims, Nicholas A., *The Diplomacy of Biological Disarmament* (London: Macmillan, 1988).

Taylor, Paul, and A. J. R. Groom (eds), *International Institutions at Work* (London: Pinter, 1988).

Taylor, Paul, *International Organisation in the Modern World* (London: Pinter, 1993).

Taylor, Richard, *Against the Bomb* (Oxford: Clarendon Press, 1988).

Thant, U [Maung], *View from the UN* (London and Newton Abbot: David & Charles; New York: Doubleday, 1978).

United Nations Department of Public Information, *The Blue Helmets – A review of United Nations Peace-Keeping*, second edn (New York: UN, 1990).

United Nations Department of Public Information, *United Nations Peace-Keeping* (New York: UN, 1993).

Urquhart, Brian, *Hammarskjöld* (London: Bodley, 1972).

Urquhart, Brian, *A Life in Peace and War* (London: Weidenfeld & Nicolson, 1987).

Vincent, R. J., (ed.), *Foreign Policy and Human Rights Issues and Responses* (Cambridge: Cambridge University Press, 1986).

White, N. D., *The United Nations and the Maintenance of International Peace and Security* (Manchester: Manchester University Press, 1990).

Williams, D., *The System in Crisis* (New York: Hurst, 1987).

Yeselson, Abraham, and Anthony Gaglione, *A Dangerous Place: The United Nations as a weapon in world politics* (New York: Viking, 1974).

Index

167